Faculty Success
Through Mentoring

**PART OF THE AMERICAN COUNCIL ON EDUCATION
SERIES IN HIGHER EDUCATION**

Susan Slesinger, Executive Editor

Other titles in the series:

Assessment for Excellence: The Philosophy and Practice of Assessment and Evaluation in Higher Education, Second Edition
  by Alexander W. Austin and Anthony Lising Antonio

Decades of Chaos and Revolution: Showdowns for College Presidents
  by Stephen D. Nelson

College Student Retention: Formula for Student Success, Second Edition
  edited by Alan Seidman

Innovations in Higher Education: Survival of the Fittest
  by Allen M. Hoffman and Stephen D. Spangehl

Fitting Form to Function: A Primer on the Organization of Academic Institutions, Second Edition
  by Rudolph H. Weingartner

Learning to Lead: A Handbook for Postsecondary Administrators
  by James R. Davis

The "How To" Grants Manual: Successful Grantseeking Techniques for Obtaining Public and Private Grants
  Seventh Edition
  by David G. Bauer

Leading from the Middle: A Case-Study Approach to Academic Leadership for Associate Deans
  by Tammy Stone and Mary Coussons-Read

Higher Education Assessments: Leadership Matters
  edited by Gary L. Kramer and Randy L. Swing

Leading the Campaign: Advancing Colleges and Universities
  by Michael J. Worth

Leaders in the Labyrinth: College Presidents and the Battlegrounds of Creeds and Convictions
  by Stephen J. Nelson

Academic Turnarounds: Restoring Vitality to Challenged American Colleges/ Universities
  edited by Terrence MacTaggart

Out in Front: The College President as the Face of the Institution
    edited by Lawrence V. Weill

Community Colleges on the Horizon: Challenge, Choice, or Abundance
    edited by Richard Alfred, Christopher Shults, Ozan Jaquette, and Shelley
    Strickland

Minding the Dream: The Process and Practice of the American Community College
    by Gail O. Mellow and Cynthia Heelan

Faculty Success Through Mentoring

A Guide for Mentors, Mentees, and Leaders

Carole J. Bland, Anne L. Taylor,
S. Lynn Shollen, Anne Marie Weber-Main,
and Patricia A. Mulcahy

Published in partnership with

 American
Council on
Education™

Leadership and Advocacy

ROWMAN & LITTLEFIELD PUBLISHERS, INC.
Lanham • New York • Toronto • Plymouth, UK

Published in partnership with the American Council on Education

Published by Rowman & Littlefield Publishers, Inc.
A wholly owned subsidiary of
The Rowman & Littlefield Publishing Group, Inc.
4501 Forbes Boulevard, Suite 200, Lanham, Maryland 20706
www.rowman.com

Estover Road, Plymouth PL6 7PY, United Kingdom

British Library Cataloguing in Publication Information Available

The hardback edition of this book was previously cataloged by the Library
of Congress as follows:

Library of Congress Cataloging-in-Publication Data

Faculty success through mentoring : a guide for mentors, mentees, and
    leaders / Carole J. Bland . . . [et al.].
        p. cm. — (American Council on Education series on higher education)
    Includes bibliographical references and index.
    1. College teachers—In-service training—United States. 2. Mentoring in
    education—United States. I. Bland, Carole J.
    LB1738.F37 2009
    371.102—dc22   2008052650

ISBN 978-1-60709-066-3 (cloth : alk. paper)
ISBN 978-0-7425-6320-9 (pbk. : alk. paper)
ISBN 978-1-60709-068-7 (electronic)

∞™ The paper used in this publication meets the minimum requirements
of American National Standard for Information Sciences—Permanence of
Paper for Printed Library Materials, ANSI/NISO Z39.48-1992.

Printed in the United States of America

Dr. Carole J. Bland
photo by Scott Wyberg Photography

We dedicate this book to our dear colleague and friend, Carole Bland, who passed away on August 23, 2008, from pancreatic cancer after a struggle marked by courage, dignity, and grace.

Carole devoted her extraordinary career to the professional development and productivity of faculty, administrators, and institutions of higher education. Her passion for cultivating faculty vitality—whether through mentoring, leadership development, or institutional change—was exceeded only by her vast scholarly contributions to the same field. She leaves behind a legacy of scholarship and programs that will continue to inform and inspire faculty and administrators for years to come.

It is only fitting that this book on faculty mentoring be the capstone to Carole's professional portfolio. She herself was a generous, tireless, and truly consummate mentor—formally to some colleagues and informally to all who had the joy and privilege of working with her. This book honors Carole and will keep her spirit a living presence.

Contents

Cartoons, Figures, Photographs, and Tables

CARTOONS

FIGURES

PHOTOGRAPHS

TABLES

Preface

This book grew out of our desire to facilitate and support the work of higher education faculty. In particular, the impetus for this book was our perceived need for a mentoring guide written specifically for two audiences: higher education faculty members seeking advice on how to be effective as either a mentor or a mentee, and leaders wanting to facilitate faculty success through a mentoring program. We wanted to create a guide that was practical and scholarly, one that provided both concrete guidance and the evidence supporting this advice.

Our desire alone would not have been enough to enable us to complete this work. We were fortunate to have the support of many other people, for which we are very grateful. We particularly want to thank E. Thomas Sullivan, senior vice president for Academic Affairs and provost, University of Minnesota; and Deborah E. Powell, dean of the Medical School and assistant vice president for Clinical Affairs, both of whom believed in and provided support for this work.

We also were privileged to have had the hands-on help of others. Elizabeth Greene prepared many early drafts, ensured the accuracy of every quotation and citation, tracked down many a picture, and handled all of the copyright permissions. Ross G. Johnson, an outstanding librarian, never failed to locate a resource. Libby Frost contributed her excellent graphic design and creative layout skills. Jeni Skar wrestled the manuscript into a final form. Kathie Luby kept us organized through the whole process. Thank you all for being such priceless partners.

Several of our colleagues reviewed earlier versions of this book. These reviewers included department chairs, higher-level administrators, directors of mentoring programs, leaders in professional associations, and researchers on mentoring. Each of these reviewers provided a unique perspective. We thank all of these busy people for their time and invaluable advice. Also, we extend a special thanks to Stylus Publishing for allowing us to include in this book parts of our work published previously in their briefing series titled *Effective Practices for Academic Leaders* (Bland & Risbey, 2006).

Our families were our constant silent partners, providing unstinting support and understanding throughout the process. Thank you again and love to Dick Bland, Alix Taylor, Jim, Linda, and Janelle Shollenberger, Tim Mulcahy, and Mike and Naomi Main.

We owe a great debt of gratitude to authors of the significant research and books written on mentoring, many of whom are cited in this book. We learned from them, built on their work, and are honored to contribute to this body of literature.

CHAPTER 1

Guide To Using This Book

RATIONALE, PURPOSE, AND AUDIENCE

Few things are more essential to the success of an academic institution than vital faculty members. Vital faculty members are passionately involved in and committed to their work, committed to the goals of the institution, continually developing their teaching and research abilities, and consistently growing in and contributing to their disciplines. These faculty characteristics, while highly desirable, cannot be assumed; they must be continually nurtured over the career continuum.

Facilitating faculty vitality is, without question, one of the most important responsibilities of leaders in higher education (department chairs, deans, provosts, presidents, etc.). It is with this critical role in mind that we wrote this book on faculty mentoring. Mentoring is a highly successful, adaptable, and practical strategy for supporting a faculty member's success and satisfaction across the career span. For example, with the help of quality mentoring:

- New faculty members can better overcome professional challenges, such as establishing collaborations, accessing resources, balancing work roles, and understanding the unwritten rules of academe.
- Midcareer and senior faculty members can avoid (or quickly recover from) periods of professional stagnancy. They can also successfully negotiate career transitions, including a shift to academic administration.

Arthur Walker, Jr., professor of applied physics and mentor to Sally K. Ride, first woman in space.
Ed Souza/Stanford News Service. Reprinted with permission.

- Faculty at any career stage can learn to articulate a vision for their career, establish appropriate short- and long-term goals for achieving that vision, and select optimal strategies for meeting their goals. These same skills (visioning, strategic planning, goal setting) can be applied in new ways by faculty members who later move into an administrative role.

The purpose of this book is to assist academic leaders and faculty members who wish to use mentoring as one strategy for facilitating faculty vitality. Some of the questions addressed in this book are: How does a mentor facilitate career success? What specific features of the

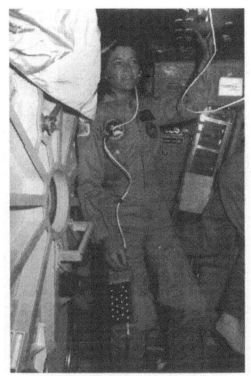

Sally K. Ride
National Aeronautics and Space Administration

mentoring relationship contribute to its effectiveness? In what ways can academic leaders best support mentoring among their faculty, particularly as faculty become more diverse? What does an effective mentoring program look like? And how does mentoring apply to faculty in mid- or late career stages, including the subset of those seeking to transition to administrative positions? This book combines research findings from the mentoring literature with practical tools for developing mentoring activities. The result is a single, evidence-based resource that can be used on an individual, departmental, or institutional level. Using effective mentoring as one strategy to attend to faculty vitality not only assists individual faculty members' success, but also better positions an institution to successfully attract and retain the best and brightest faculty to advance the organization's mission.

The intended audiences for this book are academic leaders and faculty at all levels, in any academic institution. Leaders in higher education can use this book to help train potential mentors and develop a successful, sustainable mentoring program. Although mentoring needs to be tailored to the local environment (university, professional school, department, or division), it also needs to be championed at the highest levels of leadership. Thus, this book is an essential resource for all academic leaders who seek to advocate for, develop, support, and reward mentoring in their institutions.

Individual faculty members can use this book as well. Those in a position to mentor will find it helpful to enhance their mentoring skills, and mentees seeking career guidance will be able to identify the critical elements of an effective mentoring relationship. For example, we include information to help readers understand the most important competencies that new faculty members need to acquire, such as skills in professional networking and career management. These competencies are best honed through the guidance of an experienced mentor. We include information to help faculty develop (and maintain) constructive mentoring relationships and successfully engage in career development activities appropriate to their career stage and goals. Mentors and mentees alike can apply the many principles and tools described herein to derive maximum benefit from all of their mentoring interactions.

FRAMEWORK

Throughout this book, we address two equally important and intertwined facets of mentoring. The first facet covers career development activities, while the second describes relationship development activities. This bipartite framework reflects, in part, Kram's (1985) seminal work on mentoring relationships. Kram identified two main functions of mentoring: career-enhancing functions and psychosocial functions. Career-enhancing functions "are those aspects of the relationship that enhance learning the ropes and preparing for advancement in an organization" (p. 22). Psychosocial functions "are those aspects of the relationship that enhance a sense of competence, clarity of identity, and effectiveness in a professional role" (p. 22). Mentoring can support psychosocial functions "because of an interpersonal relationship that fosters mutual trust and increasing intimacy" (p. 23).

This dual framework of the mentoring process, with both career development functions and relationship development functions, also has a basis in the known predictors of faculty productivity, satisfaction, and retention. Data demonstrate that most of the predictors of work productivity are not the same as the predictors of work satisfaction. Whereas faculty productivity is predicted by such things as drive, socialization, deep content knowledge, uninterrupted work time, a well-developed external network of colleagues, and formal training in research and teaching (Bland, Weber-Main, Lund, & Finstad, 2005), satisfaction is predicted by the intrinsic benefits (or lack thereof) of work itself: department collegiality, relations with the department chair, level of influence in the department, salary, the promotion and tenure process, autonomy, institutional recognition and support, department climate, and total amount of work time (August & Waltman, 2004; Barnes, Agago, & Coombs, 1998; Johnsrud & Des Jarlais, 1994; Manger & Eikeland, 1990; Olsen, Maple, & Stage, 1995; Smart, 1990). Most of the predictors of satisfaction—department collegiality, work climate, and local recognition, for instance—involve the existence of constructive professional relationships. Therefore, facilitating these relationships is an important component of any strategy for increasing overall faculty satisfaction.

Ideally, an institution wants to develop and retain faculty who are both productive and satisfied. The institutional investment of substantial time, effort, and dollars into career development activities is lost when highly competent and productive faculty members leave the institution because of dissatisfaction with some aspect of their work lives. Institutions often focus on strategies for promoting faculty productivity, but there is evidence that productivity does not guarantee faculty satisfaction (August & Waltman, 2004; U.S. Department of Education & National Center for Education Statistics (NCES), 2004). Moreover, satisfaction—more so than productivity—has been shown to predict retention (Johnsrud & Heck, 1994; Manger & Eikeland, 1990; Matier, 1990; Rosser, 2004; Smart, 1990). Thus, the best institutions target strategies to increase both productivity and satisfaction.

Mentoring is one of the few common predictors of both faculty productivity and satisfaction (Allen, Eby, Poteet, Lentz, & Lima, 2004; Ambrose, Huston, & Norman, 2005; Blackburn, 1979; Bland & Schmitz,

1986; Bland, Weber-Main, Lund, & Finstad, 2005; Byrne & Keefe, 2002; Cameron & Blackburn, 1981; Corcoran & Clark, 1984; Curtis, Dickinson, Steiner, Lamphear, & Vu, 2003; Dohm & Cummings, 2002; Mills, Zyzanski, & Flocke, 1995; Mundt, 2001; Roberts, 1997; Tenenbaum, Crosby, & Gliner, 2001; Wilson, Pereira, & Valentine, 2002). As such, mentoring is a crucial variable to address in order to enhance faculty productivity, satisfaction, and, consequently, retention. These findings, along with Kram's (1985) mentoring functions, highlight the mutual importance of the two critical components of the mentoring process: 1) career development activities in order to foster work productivity, and 2) relationship development activities in order to foster work satisfaction. It is common for mentors to focus quickly on the career development activities of mentoring, but effective mentoring attends to both components of the mentoring process. Doing so optimizes the likelihood of productive, satisfied faculty remaining at an institution (figure 1.1).

Another reason for attending to the relationship aspect of mentoring is to facilitate learning on the part of the mentee. Developing a learning environment that is safe and supportive, but also challenging, serves to spur work, decrease stress, and facilitate learning (Kember & Leung, 2006). For faculty mentees, the environment in which learning takes place (i.e., in which career competencies are acquired) *is* the mentoring relationship. Mentoring relationships that are characterized by high-quality communication, trust, respectful acknowledgment of differences, and other features are more conducive to learning than relationships that lack these features. It is essential that mentors and mentees interact well, so that the desired outcomes of mentoring can be achieved.

In summary, this book provides guidance on how to address two equally important facets of mentoring: career development and relationship development. Mentoring that successfully addresses both aspects will facilitate not only faculty productivity, but also faculty satisfaction—and ultimately, faculty retention and success. These are important and desirable outcomes for the mentees who are striving to develop as independent scholars and effective teachers, for the mentors who are developing their future colleagues and ensuring the continued advancement of their discipline, and for the organization that is seeking to retain faculty and develop a reputation as an institution supportive of faculty.

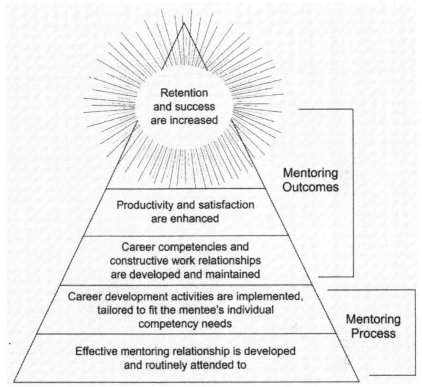

Figure 1.1.   Components and Outcomes of Effective Mentoring

CONTENT OVERVIEW

The content of this book is designed to help faculty mentors and mentees have the most effective and productive relationship. Faculty have variable experiences and success as mentors, and most are unlikely to have had the opportunity to systematically review the literature on mentoring or practices other mentors have found to be effective. We provide this information, as well as tools for mentors seeking additional strategies for effectively fulfilling their important role. In addition, many faculty may have experienced *informal* mentoring, but a *formal* approach may be new and unfamiliar. We provide an introduction to, and guidelines for, developing and implementing a more structured, formal approach to mentoring.

Many types of mentoring models can be used successfully. We give detailed attention to the "traditional" model in which an experienced and highly accomplished senior faculty member (or team of senior faculty) serves as mentor to a more junior colleague, but we also cover "alternative" mentoring models such as group and peer mentoring. Group and peer approaches may be particularly suited for addressing the needs of midcareer and senior faculty and addressing the challenges of mentoring across gender and ethnicity. In addition, group and peer mentoring models can provide a means for paying more attention to the relationship, and thus providing more psychosocial support for the mentee.

Throughout this book, we emphasize a formal, intentional approach to mentoring, in which mentor-mentee interactions are deliberate, structured, and goal-oriented. Many studies support the importance of being systematic in one's approach to mentoring. Our book both summarizes this prior literature and applies it. We describe the tangible benefits of formal mentoring in academe and other professional settings, outline the characteristics of effective mentors, mentees, and mentoring programs, and review the essential competencies that mentees will need to succeed. Further, we offer tools that institutions, mentors, and mentees can use to help faculty successfully navigate through the four phases of a mentoring relationship: preparing, negotiating, enabling, and closing.

We also provide information about how to attend to the relationship itself. This task has become more challenging as faculty become more diverse in age, gender, ethnicity, appointment type, and training. We provide a framework for mentors and mentees to learn about one another's unique challenges to career advancement and satisfaction. To this end, we include chapters explicitly focused on strategies for developing effective mentoring relationships, in general and especially across gender, ethnicity, and generation. Additionally, we devote attention to the oft-neglected mentoring needs of midcareer and senior faculty, including faculty who aspire to become academic administrators. Guidance is also provided for the leader charged with setting up a formal mentoring program.

PREVIEW OF CHAPTERS 2 THROUGH 9

- Chapter 2 begins with a working definition of faculty mentoring, and then describes its many potential benefits for mentees, mentors, and the organizations in which they work.

- Chapter 3 defines different mentoring models that can be used in higher education, identifies three overarching characteristics of effective mentoring, and suggests strategies for organizational leaders seeking to develop an effective mentoring program in their institution.
- Chapter 4 describes the needs of new faculty members, the characteristics that contribute to faculty success, and the essential role of mentoring in acquiring these characteristics.
- Chapter 5 details the four phases of the mentoring process (preparing, negotiating, enabling, and closing) and provides forms and tools to assist faculty as they proceed through each phase.
- Chapters 6 and 7 focus on establishing effective mentoring relationships, especially across gender, ethnicity, and generation.
- Chapter 8 highlights the need to support the vitality of midcareer and senior faculty members and gives examples of approaches to doing so through mentoring.
- Chapter 9 provides an overview of issues relevant to faculty members who are considering a transition to an administrative role and discusses how mentoring can help them thoughtfully manage the process.

It is best to read the chapters in sequence, as they build upon one another. Each chapter, however, addresses an important aspect of mentoring and can stand alone. We provide a section of highlights at the opening of each chapter to alert readers to the chapter's summative points.

CHAPTER 2

Definition and Benefits of Faculty Mentoring

Chapter Highlights

- *Faculty mentoring is a collaborative relationship that proceeds through purposeful stages over time. The goal of faculty mentoring is to help mentees acquire the essential competencies and constructive work relationships needed for their continued career vitality. Because mentoring can be tailored to match a mentee's particular competency needs, it can be used to support faculty at all career stages.*
- *The benefits of mentoring in the professional setting have been identified through research. For mentees, the experience of being mentored can have a positive impact on their research productivity, job satisfaction, socialization, salary levels, promotion, and teaching effectiveness. For mentors, the experience of mentoring can lead to personal satisfaction, career rejuvenation, and professional recognition.*
- *Organizations that support and encourage mentoring are likely to develop faculty who are not only highly successful (on measures such as research productivity and teaching effectiveness), but also satisfied with their overall environment and work lives. In this regard, an investment in mentoring can be expected to have a high rate of return.*

WHAT IS MENTORING?

In Homer's classic work, *The Odyssey*, when Odysseus left for the Trojan War he asked his friend, Mentor, to look after his household in his absence. Mentor provided important guidance for Odysseus's son, Telemachus, and was portrayed as a wise advisor and consistent supporter. Hence, the term *mentor* is often attributed to Homer.

Many definitions of mentoring have been applied to faculty in higher education. In this book we define faculty mentoring as a professional relationship with three essential characteristics (modified from Ritchie & Genoni, 2002, p. 69). First, mentoring is a relationship with a defined purpose: to help mentees successfully acquire the key competencies and constructive work relationships they need to lead a successful and satisfying career. The specific competencies to be gained are based on the mentee's existing abilities and career goals. Second, mentoring is a collaborative learning relationship. It is a relationship that, in the traditional model, draws upon the knowledge of suitably experienced faculty as mentors and upon the commitment of mentees to develop their professional abilities. Because the learning relationship is collaborative, other mentoring models such as peer or group mentoring (described in chapter 3) can also be used successfully. Third, mentoring is a relationship that develops over time and passes through specific phases. There is more than just a casual arrangement between the mentor and the mentee.

In academia, the role of mentee is typically assumed by the junior faculty member. Early in their career, faculty can be very challenged by the tasks of applying recently learned skills, acclimating to a new work environment and new work roles, and learning to balance their demanding teaching, research, and service duties. Experienced mentors can help new faculty overcome these challenges.

The mentee role can also be assumed by midcareer or senior faculty. Although midcareer can be a time of relative stability for faculty, it is often a time when "career recycling" occurs, with faculty adjusting to new circumstances and opportunities. Faculty who are more advanced in their careers may not require the same kind or frequency of attention offered by a traditionally structured mentoring relationship, but attention is still needed. Peer and group mentoring, a structure often favored by industry, can be beneficial for faculty who are negotiating transitions to new responsibilities or different positions, experiencing a change in family conditions, or expanding their use of new technology. Overall, attention to the needs of midcareer and senior faculty through mentoring does much to maintain their vitality and their sense of value and connection to the mission, vision, and ongoing work of their institution.

Nearly all faculty members over the course of their careers will experience a need for support, collegiality, socialization, and development. Mentoring is one of the best, most readily adaptable strategies for addressing this broad spectrum of faculty needs. As we describe next, both mentees and mentors can reap benefits from the mentoring experience. When used for ongoing faculty development, mentoring can help institutions maintain faculty members who are productive, satisfied, and committed to their profession.

BENEFITS FOR MENTEES

Much has been written about mentoring and how it can benefit working professionals in fields such as business, health, and higher education. This research—both quantitative and qualitative—has identified a diverse set of outcomes that are positively influenced by mentoring. Among these outcomes are an individual's job satisfaction, research productivity, teaching effectiveness, socialization to a profession, salary level, and career advancement. A sample of published findings in these areas is presented next.

Job and Career Satisfaction, Intention To Stay

A meta-analysis of research on mentoring in corporations showed that mentored individuals have higher satisfaction with their careers and jobs, greater intention to stay with their current organization, stronger belief that they will advance in their career, and higher commitment to their career. In addition, mentees in the later stages of the mentoring process report more benefits than those in the initiation stage, suggesting that the duration of mentoring is important (Allen et al., 2004). Similarly, in a study on faculty satisfaction, Ambrose and colleagues

(2005) found that mentoring was one of the top contributors to overall satisfaction.

Research Productivity

Numerous outcomes studies have found that having had a formal mentor is highly correlated with research productivity (Blackburn, 1979; Bland, Center, Finstad, Risbey, & Staples, 2005; Bland & Schmitz, 1986; Cameron & Blackburn, 1981; Corcoran & Clark, 1984; Curtis et al., 2003; Dohm & Cummings, 2002; Mills et al., 1995; Mundt, 2001; Paul, Stein, Ottenbacher, & Liu, 2002; Roberts, 1997; Tenenbaum et al., 2001; Wilson et al., 2002). A few illustrative examples are as follows:

- Fellows who reported having an influential mentor were more productive in publishing and in obtaining grant funding as pri-

(L-R) Dan Kleppner, mentor to David Pritchard, mentor to Wolfgang Ketterle, winner of the 2001 Nobel Prize in Physics, all from the Massachusetts Institute of Technology. Pritchard also mentored the other two 2001 winners and has mentored a total of five Nobel Prize laureates. The family tree (figure 2.1) shows these mentoring relationships.
Photo by Tom Bonnalt. Permission granted by Wolfgang Ketterle.

mary investigators than were fellows without influential mentors (Steiner, Curtis, Lanphear, Vu, & Main, 2004). Well-mentored fellows were also more likely to provide research mentorship to others.

- In a faculty sample, role-specific modeling from a mentor emerged as a predictor of research-oriented productivity (e.g., publishing and presenting, serving as principal or co-investigator on a grant, spending time on research) (Williams & Blackburn, 1988).

- According to Byrne and Keefe (2002), "in terms of scholarly productivity . . . there is no substitute for a sustained relationship grounded in research projects sponsored by one or more experts and supported by continuous resources. . . . When scholarly productivity with funded research is the desired outcome, intense involvement of a protégé with an expert researcher is essential" (pp. 395, 391).

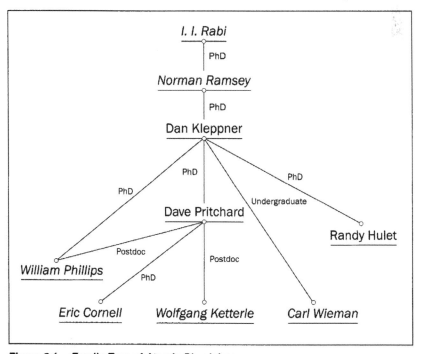

Figure 2.1. Family Tree of Atomic Physicists
Permission granted by Wolfgang Ketterle.

Teaching Effectiveness

Systematic studies of mentoring's effect on teaching are not as prevalent as studies of mentoring's effect on research activity. Many studies have investigated whether larger faculty development programs—programs that include a mentoring component—influence teaching outcomes. Although the results of these studies are generally positive, the effect of mentoring alone cannot be isolated because it is embedded in the larger development program. This does not mean, however, that mentoring is not effective for improving teaching. The following studies support the positive impact of mentoring on teaching effectiveness.

Mentoring was at the heart of the Teaching Improvement Program (TIPs) implemented at the University of Georgia. In this voluntary program, junior faculty with little teaching experience were matched with senior mentors who had reputations for being excellent teachers. After one year, 100 percent of the mentors and mentees agreed that, overall, TIPs was a valuable program. "The program appeared to help both mentors and mentees with their classroom instruction as well as encourage several participants to continue an interest in instructional improvement" (Diehl & Simpson, 1989, p. 154).

In a study of full-time faculty in schools, colleges, and departments of education in Colorado, both faculty mentees and faculty mentors reported that teaching improvements were a major outcome of mentoring (Goodwin, Stevens, & Bellamy, 1998). After participating in a structured mentoring program at the University of California, San Diego, junior faculty reported being significantly more confident in their education skills, as well as in their research and administrative abilities (Wingard, Garman, & Reznik, 2004).

Socialization To a Profession's Norms

An important role of faculty mentors is to socialize new faculty to the culture and practices (unwritten rules) of the academic profession. Corcoran and Clark (1984) compared the graduate school mentoring experiences of highly active faculty to a representative group of faculty. They found that, compared to the representative faculty group, the highly active faculty members had learned more from their professors' behaviors about what to do (and even more so, what *not* to do) in their teaching, research, and service roles. Furthermore, after the respondents had entered their first faculty positions, the highly active group continued to receive "more specific forms of encouragement such as help in obtaining subsequent positions, invitations to collaborate in research and writing, reviews and criticisms of their research and writing, and support of applications for grants and projects from their advisors" (p. 143). In contrast, the representative group of faculty continued to receive only general, informal encouragement.

Blackburn (1979) emphasized the importance of socialization and networking in this way: "Mentorship/sponsorship in the first years is critical for launching a productive career—Learning the informal network that supports productivity—the inner workings of professional associations and who the productive people are, for example—is critical" (pp. 25–26). Similarly, Ritchie and Genoni (2002) found that mentoring facilitates not only job (career) and self (psychosocial) outcomes but also professional socialization: "Mentoring introduces the protégés to and reinforces their understanding of the various standards of practice, conduct and participation which are underpinned by a set of professional values, and constitute acceptable norms within a profession" (p. 76).

Salary Levels, Salary Satisfaction, and Promotion

In a study of faculty in financial management, Melicher (2000) found that having a mentor "has a positive impact on salary levels, salary satisfaction, and promotion/tenure satisfaction" (p. 166). A study of obstetrics/gynecology fellows found that those with a mentor were more likely to be promoted (Wise et al., 2004). In addition, a meta-analysis by Allen and colleagues (2004) found that compensation and number of promotions were higher for mentored individuals than for nonmentored individuals.

BENEFITS FOR MENTORS

Mentors can also benefit from the mentoring experience. According to Ragins and Scandura (1994), mentors may derive a sense of personal

Hewlett-Packard Company founders David Packard (left) and William R. Hewlett (center) with their Stanford University engineering school mentor Fred Terman in 1952 at the door of the Hewlett-Packard wing of the Electronics Research Laboratory.
Photo courtesy of Hewlett-Packard Company

satisfaction from nurturing mentees and passing on their knowledge. Mentors' careers can be rejuvenated from exposure to the energy and ideas of mentees. In some instances, mentors might enjoy enhanced recognition from their organization for their service. Further, mentors may experience a desirable sense of loyalty from their mentees.

In a qualitative study of mentors across five types of organizations, Allen, Poteet, and Burroughs (1997) found support for many of the aforementioned mentor benefits. According to respondents, serving as a mentor gave them self-satisfaction from seeing others grow and succeed. The experience also helped them build friendships and expand their support network with new colleagues. Among the job-related benefits of mentoring were increases in the mentor's own knowledge, increases in the mentor's visibility within the organization, and the development of a competent workforce by the passing on of knowledge to others.

In a preliminary cross-sectional study, Allen, Lentz, and Day (2006) compared career success outcomes of mentors and nonmentors in a health-care organization. After controlling for demographic and human capital variables known to be associated with career success, they found that employees with experience as mentors reported a higher current salary, more promotions, and more career success than employees without experience as mentors.

In summary, prior literature indicates that both mentees and mentors can reap professional benefits from their relationship. At its best, mentoring is a collaboration, with each member contributing to the relationship and experiencing rewards.

BENEFITS FOR THE ORGANIZATION

The major benefactor of effective mentoring is the organization (Zey, 1984). The benefits experienced by the mentee and mentor collectively provide advantages to the organization, resulting in more faculty who are highly productive, creative, satisfied, and committed to their organization. For example, it is noteworthy that in a study of thirty-seven highly research-productive departments at the University of Minnesota, all of the departments that were rated in the top 5 percent of their respective fields also had formal mentoring programs (Bland, Weber-Main, et al., 2005). It is also likely that effective mentoring improves an organization's ability to recruit talented individuals and decreases turnover. Few organizations have put an actual dollar amount on the costs or benefits of mentoring. Mentoring does have its costs: "When a firm chooses to allocate its most valuable resources away from clients and to young stars, the economic consequences are real and visible" (Lorsch & Tierney, 2002, p. 73). But the potential benefits are substantial. An executive at Ernst & Young (a large professional services company) asserted that mentoring is "saving the firm $10 million annually—mainly from the cost of recruiting and training new staff" (Boyle, 2005, p. 15).

SUMMARY

Prior literature demonstrates that mentoring can be used to facilitate many positive outcomes for mentors, mentees, and organizations. It is important for higher education leaders to share findings such as these with their faculty. Doing so will provide an empirical basis for promoting faculty mentoring in their institutions. A familiarity with the scholarship on mentoring should help ensure that all faculty understand the demonstrated value of mentoring and its relevance to academe, beyond any impressions they may have acquired from their personal experience as mentors or mentees.

Mentoring can be approached in a variety of ways that are tailored to meet the needs of specific individuals and organizations. In the next chapter, we describe some of the different models for faculty mentoring. Academic leaders can adapt these models for use in their particular setting. As will be shown, institutions can design a mentoring program in such a way as to help ensure — among other things — that mentoring takes place, that the mentoring process has clear goals, that mentor-mentee teams have sufficient resources for their work together, and that all faculty bear in mind the institution's strategic priorities and vision as part of their ongoing career development.

CHAPTER 3

Mentoring Models and Effective Mentoring Programs

Chapter Highlights

- *Different types of mentoring models can be used to support faculty over the career continuum. Traditional, peer, and group are three common models. Although the models overlap in some characteristics, each has its own strengths and limitations.*
- *Mentoring models are adaptable, and multiple approaches can be used to address the needs of a diverse faculty (for example, faculty in different appointment types or at different stages of their careers).*
- *No matter what the model, mentoring is more likely to produce the desired outcomes when three criteria are met: the relationship between mentor and mentee is purposefully attended to, multiple mentors are called on for specific mentoring needs, and a formal approach to mentoring is adopted.*
- *Mentoring is more likely to occur and more likely to be effective under four conditions: when there is an institutional policy requiring mentoring, when a visible institution-wide mentoring program has been established to provide resources for unit-level programs, when units tailor the program to their faculty, and when mentoring is a valued activity.*
- *Additional features of effective mentoring programs include a clear purpose and goals, a thoughtful design (e.g., mechanism for mentor-mentee matching, training and rewards for mentors, and clear expectations), adequate resources, and routine evaluation.*

INTRODUCTION

In the previous chapter, we described some of the career-related outcomes that mentoring can influence. The summative message that emerges from the literature is that mentoring can have a wide-reaching and positive impact on faculty career development and the organizations in which they work.

Not all mentoring relationships are the same, however, and not all are equally effective. In this chapter, we describe three common mentoring models—each with its own strengths and limitations—that could be applied to faculty in higher education. We follow this overview with a description of three features that characterize *all* effective mentoring relationships, regardless of the specific model used. Further, we discuss the advantages of having an institutionally sponsored mentoring program to help support the mentoring process. Drawing from the literature, we summarize the features of an effective mentoring program. In doing so, we provide an outline for academic leaders charged with setting up a formal mentoring program in their department, college, or institution.

COMMON MENTORING MODELS

Research investigating the beneficial outcomes of mentoring (chapter 2) has almost exclusively investigated the "traditional" model, in which a senior mentor is paired with a single junior mentee. Although this is the most prevalent model, a variety of other mentoring models can be used successfully, either alone or in combination, to address multiple mentoring needs. Three models—traditional mentoring, peer mentoring, and group mentoring—are described in table 3.1 and in the text below. In this chapter we focus predominantly on defining the models and describing how they might apply to faculty in general. In chapters 8 and 9, we provide examples of how different groups of faculty (e.g., midcareer and senior faculty, faculty considering a transition to administration) might benefit from a particular type of mentoring approach.

Traditional Mentoring

The traditional approach to mentoring is likely the most familiar of the models. In this approach, an experienced senior faculty member (or

Table 3.1. Characteristics of Common Mentoring Models

Characteristic	Mentoring Model		
	Traditional	Peer	Group
Structure	hierarchical	peer	hierarchical
Format	one mentee with one mentor or a team of mentors	one-to-one or small collaborative group	one or small number of mentors with medium group of mentees
Typical career stage of mentee	early	any	early or mid
Typical career stage of mentor	mid or senior	any	mid or senior
Typical purpose and goals of the mentoring relationship	career planning and advancement socialization skill learning goal activity project centered	goal activity skill learning life issues relationship centered	career advancement socialization topic centered
Need for coordinator	high—contract, agreements, expectations, matching, nudging	medium—use of facilitator or consensus	medium—use of facilitators
Challenges	recruiting and training enough mentors to fill demand time commitment	recruiting providing training for peer mentoring time commitment changing group membership	differing needs of group members providing skill training for group interaction managing group dynamics time commitments changing group membership

Note. Adapted with permission from *A Chart Summarizing Four Different Types of Mentoring: Intentional, Traditional, Peer, and Transition,* by R. Carr, 2000. Victoria, BC: Peer Systems Consulting Group. (Retrieved September 10, 2006, from http://www.mentors.ca/Peer_Resources_Network.html/Projects).

a team of senior faculty members) facilitates the career development of a junior faculty member. The mentor-mentee relationship is primarily hierarchical. This arrangement offers clear advantages to the mentee, who can benefit from the extensive knowledge, organizational wisdom, contacts, sponsorship, and experience that come from working with a senior colleague.

The traditional approach does have limitations. One potential difficulty is finding a sufficient number of trained senior mentors, particularly senior women and minority faculty members, who are willing and able to serve in this role. This can be a significant issue in smaller departments and even in large departments that have an imbalanced proportion of senior to junior faculty. Another concern is the situation in which the mentee reports only and directly to the mentor, or when the mentee is directly involved in the mentor's academic work (e.g., team-teaching a course or being part of the mentor's research team). In these situations, there is the possibility of a conflict of interest, which could lead to exploitation of the mentee. (We give greater attention to ineffective mentoring practices in chapter 5 and to power differentials in chapter 6.) Another possible drawback to traditional mentoring is perpetuation of the status quo. This occurs when mentors guide junior faculty to "maintain things as they are." Although academic socialization is important for sustaining the basic values and tenets of academe, it may inadvertently perpetuate systems that no longer fit the times or that hinder the success of new faculty who have different backgrounds and expectations.

Using a team of senior mentors to provide multiple viewpoints and to address multiple mentoring needs can protect against many of these limitations to traditional mentoring. Indeed, the need for multiple mentors is one of the common characteristics of effective mentoring that we will discuss later in this chapter. In addition, we provide specific strategies for addressing the challenges of mentoring across gender, ethnicity, and generation in chapters 6 and 7.

Peer Mentoring

Like traditional mentoring, peer mentoring has always existed. With this approach, a pair or small group of faculty, all at similar career stages, gather for the purpose of mutual career development and support. According to Kram and Isabella (1985), "the lack of the hierarchical dimension in a peer relationship might make it easier to achieve communication, mutual support, and collaboration" (p. 112). By fostering collaborations, peer mentoring can provide the beginnings of a network that will serve faculty well over an entire career. (The importance of building professional networks—which are somewhat different and go beyond networks of peers—is discussed in chapter 4.)

In contrast to traditional mentoring relationships, which are primarily hierarchical, peer mentoring is based on mutuality (Kram & Isabella, 1985). Peer relationships "provide a forum for mutual exchange in which an individual can achieve a sense of expertise, equality, and empathy that is frequently absent from traditional mentoring relationships" (p. 129). Peer relationships can also be a safe place for junior faculty to develop without the scrutiny of senior faculty. For early career faculty, a peer mentoring approach can add a helpful dimension when used in tandem with a traditional approach. The peer approach is also discussed in chapters 8 and 9, as it may be of particular value to midcareer and senior faculty and faculty considering a transition to academic administration.

The chief limitation of peer mentoring is that it does not offer the junior mentee the many substantial benefits that come from working with a senior mentor. Both models provide career-enhancing benefits, but the traditional model—in which the mentor has the ability to sponsor, open doors to major committees, make introductions to other established senior faculty, and transmit critical career enhancing knowledge to the mentee—can more effectively move a career forward.

Recently, attention has been given to using a peer mentoring program as an alternative or supplement to traditional mentoring. Studies have been conducted on a formal peer mentoring approach for faculty called a Collaborative Mentoring Program (Pololi & Knight, 2005; Pololi, Knight, Dennis, & Frankel, 2002). This approach uses a group facilitator and ". . . a group process characterized by nonhierarchical peer relationships, protégé(e) empowerment, and self-direction. This reflective process involves the self-identification of personal and professional goals that are consistent with an individual's personal values" (Pololi & Knight, 2005, p. 866). Pololi and colleagues (2002) reported that participants perceived several advantages of formal peer mentoring compared to traditional mentoring. They found it easier to communicate with peers than with senior faculty; they found comfort in the realization that their peers were facing similar issues; they were able to establish supportive social and professional networks; and they were exposed to multiple perspectives and thus able to match themselves with peers who were a good fit.

CompanyCommand is another example of the use of peer mentoring. This approach makes use of "an internal U.S. Army Web site where junior officers facing professional challenges can seek advice from others who have been in similar situations" (Dixon, 2006, p. 56). Developed initially by two junior officers serving as company commanders for the first time, this Web site supplements advice from senior officers whose experiences may not match current battle situations.

Group Mentoring

Group mentoring differs from pure peer mentoring in that it has a designated leader(s), usually a senior person in the field. "It is posited that within a group mentoring programme the mentoring functions and roles of conventional, individual mentoring relationships could be shared by the group's facilitators . . . and through the development of peer mentoring relationships within the group" (Ritchie & Genoni, 2002, p. 71). Group mentoring offers many of the benefits of traditional and peer mentoring, such as exposure of mentees to multiple perspectives, access to the wisdom and networks of more senior mentors, and support from peers at similar career stages.

Group mentoring has been embraced by law firms as a development strategy for junior members (Abbott, 2000). "Group mentoring pairs a small number of experienced lawyers with a larger number of lawyers who have less experience. The typical mentoring group consists of two mentors and five or six mentees. Mentoring groups allow firms to leverage available mentors, give young lawyers access to a larger number of lawyers in the firm, and enable mentors to share responsibility for leading mentoring activities" (Abbott, 2006, para. 25).

Ritchie and Genoni (2002) studied a group mentoring approach used by the Australian Library and Information Association to facilitate the transition of new librarians into the profession. The study included sixty-three new librarians who either participated in a group mentoring experience, were mentored in a traditional (individual) model, or had no mentoring. The group mentoring model consisted of eleven two-hour, monthly meetings with a group mentor and guest presentations. Group mentoring, compared to the other forms, resulted in significantly better outcomes in the areas of career development and professionalism, but not on psychosocial outcomes (e.g., subjects' perceptions of belonging to the profession, being involved in their peer support network, having belief in their knowledge and ability to apply skills, and awareness of issues affecting their work and profession).

Variations on the Common Models

The Collaborative Mentoring Program (CMP) reported on above (Pololi & Knight, 2005; Pololi et al., 2002) perhaps could be classified as a group mentoring format, rather than peer mentoring. The difference is that the typical group mentoring format is led by a team of senior faculty with experience and expertise that is similar to the future career plans of the junior members of the group. In the CMP model, the group facilitator may or may not have had this background.

Another variation on the models is mentoring circles. Sometimes the term "mentoring circles" is simply another term for group mentoring as defined above. It can also refer to a small number of faculty who differ in terms of age, experience, and status, meeting together to learn from one another as they explore shared interests. Usually the impetus for a mentoring circle is the need to address a common goal, such as learning a Web-based approach to teaching, or the need to navigate a common career step, such as promotion or retirement. Unlike mentoring groups, which are generally led by mentors, mentoring circles are typically led by a single member of the circle. Alternatively, leadership responsibility is rotated among members of the circle.

These examples point out that although there are "common" models, there are many possible variations. It is important to select, or create, the mentoring approach that is the best fit, by considering the needs of the faculty involved and the resources available.

Use of Multiple Models

Some institutions have adopted multiple mentoring approaches for the same group of faculty. For example, Pierce (1998) reported on a yearlong mentoring approach for new faculty at a public teaching university (Montclair State University) called the New Faculty Program. The approach has two components: First, each faculty member is assigned an individual mentor. Second, the mentors together facilitate a weekly two-hour group session for the entire cohort. The thought is that "the group can be a significant supplemental source of support and learning for new faculty and increases the likelihood that needs will be met when coupled with the one-on-one relationship with mentors" (para. 27).

Some organizations have crafted different mentoring models to meet the needs of people at different career stages. An example is Ernst & Young, a global organization that "provides a range of services, including accounting and auditing, tax reporting and operations, tax advisory, business risk services, technology and security risk services, transaction advisory, and human capital services" (Ernst & Young, 2007). This organization began a mentoring program in their tax and audit division as a means of increasing the success of women and minorities. Women with less than five years of experience received one-on-one mentoring with a partner from their department. Those with more than five years of experience were mentored via a group approach, which entailed six or seven mentees meeting with a three-person senior team that included a partner and a woman. In 2002, they launched a Learning Partnerships program that pairs minority employees with senior leadership. In addition, their Executive Mentoring Program pairs high-potential minority partners with members of Ernst & Young's Americas Executive Board (Boyle, 2005). This systematic use of multiple tailored mentoring approaches illustrates how this strategy can be used to facilitate career success.

In academe, colleges and departments might find it helpful to use multiple mentoring models to best support their faculty. One department known to the authors uses three approaches to mentoring: traditional, group, and mentoring circles. The department has set up a traditional approach in which a team of senior mentors is assigned to work with each junior faculty member hired into a research-oriented appointment. A group approach is used for faculty appointed on a newly established appointment type that has equal emphasis on scholarship and teaching. This approach was selected because, as yet, only a few senior faculty have had the experience of progressing up the career ladder in this appointment type. A senior faculty member does, however, facilitate the group. In addition, a new mentoring circle has been established by the most senior faculty to discuss and share information on planning for their next career stage or retirement.

THREE OVERARCHING CHARACTERISTICS OF EFFECTIVE MENTORING

Regardless of the mentoring model selected, effective mentoring relationships all have some characteristics in common. Here, we highlight three such characteristics that are identified as important in the literature:

1. The quality of the mentoring relationship matters and must be attended to for optimal learning to occur and for high career satisfaction to be achieved.
2. Whenever possible, mentees should have multiple mentors in order to gain multiple perspectives and a variety of types of support.
3. A formal, intentional approach to the mentoring experience is most likely to succeed. A formal approach is one in which mentor-mentee interactions are deliberate, structured, and goal-oriented.

We discuss each of these overarching characteristics of effective mentoring next.

Quality Relationship

We first noted in chapter 1 that attention to developing the mentoring relationship itself is the foundation of a successful mentoring experience. Ragins, Cotton, and Miller (2000) found that, among 1,162 employees in social work, engineering, and journalism, satisfaction with a mentoring relationship was the most powerful predictor of job and career attitudes. Notably, they also found that when the mentoring relationship was unsatisfactory, the impact on job and career attitudes was more negative than the impact of not having a mentoring relationship.

For mentoring to be successful, it is essential to establish a purposeful, positive, constructive relationship—one that will facilitate learning for the mentee and promote his or her overall satisfaction. With this in mind, we include information in other chapters regarding how to set learning goals for the mentee, activities to support these goals, and proactive ways to establish and maintain a good mentoring relationship. These strategies include, for example, establishing trust, communicating openly and often, recognizing power differentials, understanding generational differences, and responding to potential challenges to success—including challenges that can significantly affect women and ethnic minorities.

Multiple Mentors

A single formally assigned mentor may not be able to meet every need of a mentee. Thus, it is ideal for a faculty member to have more than one mentor. Multiple mentors can provide mentees with different perspectives and a variety of types of support (Higgins & Thomas, 2001; Levinson, Kaufman, Clark, & Tolle, 1991; Peluchette & Jeanquart, 2000; Thomas, 2001).

On the one hand, it can be helpful for mentors and mentees to have some commonalities. For example, mentees might find that having a mentor of the same ethnicity, age, or gender is useful for overcoming specific challenges related to that demographic. A faculty member might benefit from being able to discuss work-life balance with a mentor who shares a similar family structure (for example, has significant caregiving responsibilities or is in a long-distance relationship). Faculty with the same training background (PhD versus MD) and research focus might be well suited for working together as mentor and mentee.

On the other hand, there is much to be learned from a mentor who differs from the mentee, be that in demographics, academic discipline,

Joshua Lederberg (Nobel laureate and genetics researcher), mentor to Carl Sagan (astrophysicist and writer).
The Joshua Lederberg Papers, Professional Photographs. Profiles in Science, National Library of Medicine. (Joshua Lederberg at the Kennedy Space Center, August, 7, 1975.)

work habits, leadership style, or other characteristics. In these situations, the mentoring relationship might serve to challenge the mentee in positive ways, prompting growth and advancement in areas that would not be addressed otherwise. Some of the best mentors may be outside the department or even the institution. Still, it is important for a faculty member to have at least one local mentor from his or her home department or division. This will ensure that the mentee is acculturated to the particular norms, governance structure, goals, and values that characterize his or her discipline and immediate work unit.

Although faculty members may be formally assigned only one mentor, they should be encouraged to seek out additional mentors, either formal or informal, to receive support in the many dimensions of faculty life. The formally assigned mentor can be a great help in identifying other suitable mentors.

Gerald Kuiper (astronomer), mentor to Carl Sagan (astrophysicist and writer).
Reprinted with permission of the Lunar and Planetary Laboratory, University of Arizona.

Formal Approach

All of the mentoring models described in this chapter can occur informally or formally. However, the literature shows that a formal approach can provide the intended benefits more consistently than an informal approach. For example, a study of medical school faculty at the University of Minnesota–Twin Cities found that having or having had a formally designated mentor was the second-best predictor of high research productivity (having a passion for research was first); however, this association did not hold when the mentoring relation-

Dr. Carl Sagan relaxes outside the Space Sciences Building at Cornell University.
Photo by Michael Okoniewski, copyright 1994. Reprinted with permission.

ship was informal or nonstructured (Bland, Seaquist, Pacala, Center, & Finstad, 2002).

Certainly, many a faculty member has benefited from informal mentoring. But Boyle and Boice (1998) found that informal mentoring is less likely to occur spontaneously for minority faculty or women faculty. Similarly, Ragins and Cotton (1991) found that women face more barriers to developing informal mentoring relationships than do men. Further, the attention given to systematic mentoring and the outcomes of mentoring are likely to be more variable for informal approaches.

Other studies echo the importance of being systematic in one's approach to mentoring, for example:

- Wilson, Pereira, and Valentine (2002), in their examination of social work faculty, report that mentoring programs must be "carefully developed and supported if protégés, mentors, and their organizations are to fully realize these benefits. Factors such as mentor-protégé matching, mentor characteristics, the roles of mentors, organizational support, and the mentoring process must be considered if a successful mentoring program is to be implemented" (p. 317).
- Drotar and Avner (2003) add, "Prospective faculty mentors (and departmental chairs) need to recognize that mentoring is a rewarding privilege of academic life that demands protected time, energy, and extraordinary commitment, which cannot and should not be made by everyone" (p. 2).
- Boyle and Boice (1998) found that mentoring is not dependent on personality, but rather on tasks and activities that the mentor and mentee do together. They reported that early and enduring mentoring is most beneficial; that mentoring pairs/teams do meet regularly and progress when given "nudging;" and that to be most beneficial, mentoring programs require a coordinator. Three other findings from their work warrant special mention: Using mentors from outside the mentee's department is very effective; less than 25 percent of faculty find mentors on their own (those who do are most often white men); and formal mentoring is, overall, more effective than informal.
- Morzinski, Diehr, Bower, and Simpson (1996) showed that a formal mentoring program improved the development of professional academic skills of junior family medicine faculty. Professional academic skills were defined according to Bland, Schmitz, Stritter, Henry, and Aluise (1990) as knowing how to manage one's career; understanding the values, norms, and expectations of academic medicine; and developing and maintaining a productive network of colleagues. In addition, longer participation in the program was associated with greater gains.

These examples highlight an important point: A formal approach to mentoring goes well beyond the step of "assigning a mentor." To provide the intended benefits, a formal approach also includes thoughtful planning about how mentees and mentors are connected, the purpose of the mentoring effort (including the specific competencies to be gained by the mentee), monitoring and evaluation, a coordinator, and more (Wanberg, Kammeyer-Mueller, & Marchese, 2006; Wanberg, Welsh, & Hezlett, 2003). A haphazard, minimal effort at a formal approach does not provide added benefits over informal mentoring and could even negatively impact the mentee (Hezlett & Gibson, 2005). This leads to our final topic for this chapter, the value of supporting faculty mentoring through a well-designed, institutionally sponsored program.

SETTING UP AN EFFECTIVE MENTORING PROGRAM

The need for organizations to support the continual evolution of their workforce is well recognized in the corporate world. The business literature estimates that "50% of employees' skills become outdated within three to five years" (Moe & Blodget, 2000, p. 229). As a result, this literature also estimates that the high-performance workplace will require workers to spend as much as 20 percent of their time in formal education to upgrade their knowledge and skills (Duderstadt, 2001). In academe as well, there is a persistent need for institutions to support the continual development of their faculty. This is especially true during times of high faculty turnover and faculty shortages. Although the addition of faculty from outside the institution is a healthy occurrence, the influx of new faculty over the next ten years will be particularly great as the baby boomer generation of faculty retires. For example, Cornell University alone reports needing to hire four hundred new faculty during 2006–2011 (Steele, 2006). When faculty turnover is high, institutions carry the heavy responsibility of simultaneously socializing new faculty while retaining and maintaining the abilities and satisfaction of veteran faculty (Bland & Bergquist, 1997). Mentoring is an excellent strategy for doing this.

Recruiting the best faculty for a particular position is costly in time and money. The actual cost will vary by institution type and discipline, but here are some examples. A 2004 study of mentoring in the medical school at the University of California, San Diego estimated recruitment costs (e.g., interviews, travel, and meals) to be $10,000–$15,000. Further, the "startup costs [not including salary] ranged from $250,000–$400,000 for a junior basic scientist to $150,000–$300,000 for a junior nonbench scientist" (Wingard, Garman, & Reznik, 2004, p. S10). Other studies report a similar average start-up cost, $250,000, to hire a junior medical school faculty member (e.g., Demmy, Kivlahan, & Stone, 2002). Cornell University estimates the start-up costs of a new faculty member to be "$100,000-plus in the humanities to more than $1 million in engineering" (Steele, 2006, p. 1). Each year these numbers increase with inflation. In addition, these numbers do not describe the total cost of recruiting new faculty, which also include a salary, space, staff support, and more. Further, when the new recruit is replacing a faculty member who has left for another institution, there is a high likelihood that the salary for the new recruit will be higher than that of the faculty member who left. For example, Hobbs, Weeks, and Finch (2005) found "the premiums required for replacing finance faculty members at all ranks are substantial" (p. 253)—even when replacing one faculty member with another of the same rank. Their study of 356 U.S. colleges and schools of business administration found that replacing an assistant professor with a new assistant professor costs an additional $10,000 in annual salary. The average premium for replacing an associate professor with a new associate professor was $18,333 and for replacing a full professor with a new full professor was $27,599. A mentoring program can help decrease these costs by increasing an institution's ability to both attract and retain faculty (Wingard et al., 2004).

Other forces besides a shifting faculty profile are driving the need for faculty development. For example, higher education in the United States is faced with increased competition from a global market and Web-based instruction. Faculty are continually challenged to adapt to rapid changes in knowledge and technology. As a result, higher education institutions must redefine themselves, and faculty members must routinely participate in developmental activities to keep pace (Bland & Risbey, 2006).

Mentoring is one way to facilitate the continued development and success of faculty at all stages—new, midcareer, and senior. We emphasize here that for faculty mentoring to be highly effective, it needs to be facilitated and supported by the organization itself. Certainly, it is possible for a mentoring relationship to be established and maintained without support from the organization. However, mentoring in this fashion can require considerable initiative on the part of both the mentee and mentor. The mentee must first actively seek out one or more mentors who have expertise and experience that aligns with his or her career goals. This task alone can be difficult for a new faculty member coming into an institution without a strong familiarity with local colleagues. Then, once a mentor has been identified and has agreed to serve in the role, both mentor and mentee must be self-motivated to keep the relationship vital, working together to ensure that they are interacting frequently enough and in useful, productive ways. At any point along the way, any number of challenges can derail the process: lack of clear, agreed upon expectations; time pressures; lack of recognition or rewards for being a mentor; or departure of the mentor from the institution.

Fortunately, leadership in many higher education departments, divisions, and schools recognizes these difficulties and the unpredictability of informal mentoring. In response, they have proactively established and supported mentoring programs to help ensure faculty success. An institutionally sponsored mentoring program can offer many resources to individual mentor-mentee dyads or teams: training and recognition for mentors, facilitated access for mentees to other career development activities within the institution, and tools for goal setting and evaluation of the mentee's progress. In addition, when mentoring is positioned within a larger program, it is more likely to receive visible support from administrators and to link the individual goals of the mentored faculty to the goals of the larger institution in a tangible way.

Figure 3.1 provides a list of eight essential features of an effective traditional mentoring program. These characteristics emerged from our synthesis of the literature on this topic. Although most of the available literature assumed that the program would support a traditional model of mentoring, many of these program features are also applicable to peer and group approaches. Next, we provide a brief description of each feature to assist administrators charged with developing or modifying a mentoring program in their institution.

1. **Program has a clearly stated purpose and goals.**
   - Purposes and goals are agreed upon by all principles (e.g., director, coordinator, sponsor, mentors) of the program.
   - Purposes and goals are consistent with larger organizations goals and culture.

2. **Program has support of faculty and administrators.**
   - Program enjoys visible support from administrators.
   - Faculty feel a shared ownership of the program.

3. **Program is positioned appropriately within the larger organization.** This will depend on the scope of the program (e.g., part of an initiative, internal to a department, college-wide). It is important to tailor the mentoring to the field or discipline of the mentee. Thus, programs positioned at a level higher than a department will likely provide guidelines and serve as a resource to mentoring programs tailored to lower level units, e.g., assisting in tailoring department programs, providing mentor training and support, providing mentoring materials.

4. **Program design, ideally, includes the following elements or features:**
   - For each mentee, formal initiation and ending of program
   - Stated qualifications for mentors
   - Mechanism for matching mentors and mentees
   - Identified person or team of mentors for each mentee
   - Training for mentors and mentees
   - Recognition for mentors' effort, e.g., in promotions, financial incentives, mini-sabbatical, awards
   - Clear expectations for each mentor, or mentor team and each mentee, including outcomes to be achieved via mentoring and timing and type of strategies used to achieve these outcomes
   - In addition to common expectations across all mentor team/mentee pairs, each pair/team commits to a mentoring agreement which lists goals and activities specific to that mentee
   - Program wide activities to support mentors and mentees (e.g., teaching workshops, grant writing workshops, writing seminar, Web-based materials on HIPAA, Responsible Conduct of Research, promotion and tenure guidelines, human subjects proposals)
   - Regular meetings of mentor/mentor team and mentee
   - Systematic contact of coordinator with mentors and mentees to trouble shoot, provide assistance and monitor progress
   - Mechanism for mentor/mentor teams and mentee arrangements to change, when appropriate
   - A timeline for mentoring which indicates the end of the formal program, although mentor/mentee relationships may continue

5. **Program is evaluated** both to assure that program elements are being implemented as planned and to assess if the program and individual mentee goals are being achieved.

6. **Program is linked and coordinated with other similar programs** such as ones at other levels of the organization or for specific groups (e.g., women, minorities, faculty development).

7. **Program has a clearly stated administrative structure.** For example, a coordinator is named, the person to whom the coordinator and program report is identified, sponsors/advocates/patrons are identified, an advisory committee is established (if appropriate).

Figure 3.1.   Characteristics of an Effective Mentoring Program

1. The program has a clearly stated purpose and goals.

It is important to the success of any program that the purpose and goals are agreed upon by all principals. In the case of a faculty mentoring program, the likely principals would be the organizational leaders (dean, department chair, or division director), mentoring program director, coordinator, sponsor, and of course, mentors and mentees. The purpose of most faculty mentoring programs is to facilitate faculty success—develop and increase teaching, research, and service effectiveness and productivity. Beyond this overall purpose, it is important that the specific goals of the program be consistent with the goals and culture of the larger organization. For example, consider an institution that has completed a major strategic planning effort and focused its vision on being among the top ten research institutions. In this context, the goals of a mentoring program might include ensuring that faculty are aware of the new institutional focus, helping mentees assess whether this focus matches their individual career visions, and then specifically supporting individual faculty in their efforts to achieve high research productivity. A mentoring program should also transmit important elements of the institutional culture. For example, the culture may be based on a shared commitment to social justice or a belief in the benefits of multidisciplinary education and research. In the latter case, a goal of the mentoring program might be to connect mentees with faculty in related disciplines in order to foster multidisciplinary work.

2. *The program is supported and valued by faculty and leadership.*

Visible support for mentoring from executive leadership is essential. Senior leaders need to demonstrate their commitment to the mentoring program in tangible ways and hold the program accountable for facilitating faculty success. Serving as mentors themselves is a powerful way for administrators to model the importance of mentoring and demonstrate their vested interest in it. Executive leaders are responsible for ensuring that the mentoring program has an effective leader and any necessary program infrastructure. Perhaps most important, leaders must find ways to enable and reward the time spent by senior faculty on mentoring.

It is equally important that the faculty themselves are committed to supporting a successful mentoring program. It is their time that is needed to make mentoring operational. Because faculty have significant control of their time, it is important that they consider mentoring a worthwhile and valued activity. To this end, faculty need to believe in the benefits of mentoring and be involved in the decision to use mentoring to support the development of their colleagues and the future of their discipline.

In some departments, mentoring is an ingrained activity. Senior faculty do not expect specific rewards for mentoring, but rather see it as one of their essential "service activities," such as serving on promotion and tenure committees, writing letters of recommendation for students seeking admission to graduate programs, or reviewing materials and writing external letters of recommendation for faculty seeking promotion in other institutions. More recently, however, mentoring has been considered a "teaching" task that should be counted, evaluated, and rewarded like other teaching activities. When this is the case, time spent on mentoring and evidence of effectiveness can be included in annual reviews and salary decisions and in documents for promotion decisions. Institutions could create awards to recognize excellence in faculty mentoring. In some cases, when a mentor is included on a grant application, a percentage of the mentor's salary can be included in the budget to cover the cost of time spent mentoring.

3. *The program is positioned appropriately within the larger organization, and tailored to fit each academic unit.*
Mentoring programs are more likely to be effective under four conditions:

- When there is an institutional policy requiring mentoring;
- When a visible institution-wide mentoring program has been established to provide resources for unit-level programs;
- When units tailor the program to their faculty; and
- When mentoring is a valued activity.

Even a well-intentioned mentoring effort—one with substantial institutional support—can quickly become expendable when other pressures arise. An institutional mentoring policy can protect against such erosion. A policy also makes visible the important element of leadership support described above and provides a clear signal to both existing faculty and recruits that the institution values and supports its faculty.

Institutional support for mentoring at the highest levels is essential. This is accomplished by establishing an institution-wide program and placing the responsibility for and coordination of the mentoring program high in the organizational structure. Simultaneously, higher-level institutional leaders need to publicly and frequently express the importance of and their support for the program. (We discuss this more under point seven.)

Although high-level institutional support is essential, it is equally important that the details related to the design and implementation of a mentoring program are decided at the local level. Mentoring strategies are most effective when they can be tailored to individual and departmental needs. In their book on highly research-productive departments, Bland, Weber-Main, Lund, and Finstad (2005) reported that "highly research-productive departments use a multitude of diverse mentoring strategies in accordance with their size, diversity, geographic proximity, and so on. But always, mentoring is valued, expected, and facilitated in one or more ways" (p. 79).

The different mentoring models described above can serve as a platform for designing the strategies that best fit each department. For example, a well-established department with significant numbers of successful senior faculty might use a traditional approach in which each new faculty member is formally paired with one or more senior mentors. This same department might use a peer mentoring approach to support its more senior faculty members. In another department that consists mostly of junior faculty, a group approach may be needed, with assistance from senior faculty in other departments to serve as mentors for their new faculty cohorts.

4. *The program design, ideally, includes the following elements or features* (as shown in figure 3.1):

- Formal starting point for each mentee and mentor team that indicates the start of the formal program.
- Stated qualifications for mentors, with attention to the potential mentor's background, mentoring competencies, and willingness to serve in the role.
- Mechanism for matching mentors and mentees, wherein each has a voice in the match.
- Identified person or team of mentors for each mentee.
- Training for mentors and mentees.

- Recognition for mentors' efforts (e.g., through promotions, financial incentives, mini-sabbaticals, and awards).
- Clear expectations for each mentor and mentee, including outcomes to be achieved via mentoring and timing and type of strategies used to achieve these outcomes.
- Commitment of each mentor-mentee team to a mentoring agreement that lists goals and activities specific to that mentee.
- Program-wide activities to support mentors and mentees (e.g., teaching workshops, grant writing workshops, writing seminars, Web-based materials, Responsible Conduct of Research, promotion and tenure guidelines, and human subjects proposals).
- Regular meetings of mentor-mentee teams.
- Systematic contact of coordinator with mentors and mentees to troubleshoot, provide assistance, and monitor progress.
- Mechanism for mentor-mentee teams to change, when appropriate.
- Formal endpoint for each mentoring relationship, which indicates the end of the formal program (although mentoring relationship may continue informally).

Many of these design elements are discussed further in other chapters of this book.

5. The program is evaluated.

Evaluation is an essential component of any mentoring program. A well-developed and implemented evaluation plan will serve several purposes. First, it will ensure that program elements are being implemented as planned. Second, it will assess if the program's and mentees' goals are being achieved. Evaluation findings should be disseminated appropriately. In particular, the accomplishments of the mentoring program must be made known to faculty and administrators in order to maintain ongoing support and financial resources to run the program.

6. The program is linked and coordinated with other similar programs.

Institutions often have related programs aimed at facilitating faculty success. Such programs may be administered at other levels of the organization and targeted to specific groups (e.g., women, minorities) or focused on specific institutional priorities, such as Web-based instruction or multidisciplinary education. Linking and coordinating a mentoring program with these other programs helps to connect mentoring teams with broader resources and to integrate the mentoring program into the institution. It is particularly wise to collaborate with other related programs in the case of minority faculty. Often, minority faculty will be joining departments in which they are the only minority or the only person of their specific ethnicity. Although it is not necessary that minority faculty be matched with senior minority faculty, minorities do face unique challenges that someone with a similar background may be best able to help them navigate (see chapter 6). Looking to the larger organization for additional resources will help the mentor identify and connect his or her mentee with successful faculty who share similar backgrounds.

7. The program has a clearly stated administrative structure.

A successful mentoring program requires a leader who is knowledgeable about mentoring, is able to attend to the many tasks involved in setting up a mentoring program, and can provide oversight for the entire initiative. It may be possible to do this with co-leaders or a committee. Regardless, it is clearly essential to identify the program leader(s), other program staff, program resources, and an advisory committee. An advisory committee that includes mentors, mentees, an ombudsperson, and organizational leaders can provide a valuable sounding board for the mentoring program leadership. These advisors can also be the means by which news about the mentoring program (evaluation results and design changes) is shared with critical constituencies and by which program accountability is strengthened.

8. Needed program resources are identified and provided by leadership.

Resources for a mentoring program might include staff (number, qualifications, and time committed), space, number and types of mentors and rewards (e.g., honoraria, recognition, and release time), workshop expenses, and technology. Program success will be facilitated by the availability of easy to use technological tools, such as Web sites, project management software, and group work sites. The finances needed to fund a mentoring program will vary greatly by the size of the program. Also, the costs may be spread across the organization if there is a decentralized approach. Whatever the resource level, it is important to make a long-term commitment because setting up an effective mentoring program takes some time and the outcomes may not be apparent in the short term. If a decentralized approach is taken, the academic units need assurance that the central commitment is solid and ongoing if they are to commit their resources to mentoring.

In summary, the likelihood of mentoring occurring and being effective is greatly increased by the establishment of a mentoring program that carefully attends to the eight elements discussed above. Zachary (2005) succinctly points out the benefits of establishing a mentoring infrastructure: "Infrastructure brings organizational mentoring to life. It is indispensable to . . . implement mentoring coherently, comprehensively, and conscientiously" (p. 57).

For readers seeking more information on establishing a mentoring program, Appendix A contains a useful list of questions to consider when setting up a mentoring program and provides a checklist for assessing infrastructure components described here. In addition, the Peer Resources Web site is a rich and continually growing information source on mentoring (http://www.mentors.ca/peer.html).

CHAPTER 4

Mentoring New Faculty Members

Chapter Highlights

- *New faculty face many challenges as they embark on their careers. Their concerns can include finding the time, resources, colleagues, rewards, and work-life balance needed for career success and satisfaction. Mentors are important allies in averting or confronting these potential sources of faculty stress and dissatisfaction.*
- *Besides problem solving, mentors are called upon to help new faculty acquire the essential competencies (e.g., in research, teaching, administration, and communication) that are known contributors to success in academe.*
- *Mentors should consider not only areas of needed growth for the individual mentee, but also other powerful predictors of an individual faculty member's vitality—specifically, the characteristics of the mentee's work environment (department or division) and the leadership of that environment. Institutional characteristics can greatly help or hinder the success of its members.*
- *One of the most important responsibilities of a mentor is to socialize a new faculty member to the academic profession. The socialized faculty member knows how to manage a career to professionally advance in the academy, understands academic values, and is successful at establishing and maintaining a productive network of academic colleagues.*

INTRODUCTION

Up to this point, we have focused our discussion on three big-picture topics: the power of mentoring to positively influence faculty productivity, satisfaction, and retention; the features, both shared and unique, of some of the most prevalent mentoring models; and the role of academic leaders in setting up a formal faculty mentoring program. With this background in place (chapters 2 and 3), we now turn our attention to the *content* of the mentoring relationship—important areas of professional development that are typically addressed in the mentoring of new faculty members.

To help new faculty members succeed, mentors are called upon to help mentees identify and achieve their own *unique* career objectives as well as the goals of their organization. In addition, mentors need to be knowledgeable about the many *general* factors that can inhibit or contribute to the sustained vitality of any faculty member. These general factors are the subject of this chapter.

We begin by describing some of the general obstacles commonly experienced by new faculty—areas of work stress and dissatisfaction that need to be successfully managed during a faculty member's first critical years in the profession. We then summarize the general factors that contribute to faculty success. These factors include essential *individual* characteristics that mentors can help mentees acquire, as well as essential *institutional* and *leadership* characteristics that, by their presence or absence, can greatly influence a faculty member's vitality.

In the second half of the chapter, we focus on an important subset of the essential individual faculty competencies, which we call the professional academic competencies. These include managing one's career, understanding academic values and behavior codes, and establishing a professional network. We focus on these professional academic competencies for two reasons. First, they can have a profound influence on a faculty member's satisfaction and productivity. Second, mentoring is one of the best strategies for socializing new faculty to the profession, thereby helping them to acquire these essential competencies with greater ease.

OBSTACLES TO FACULTY SUCCESS

The life of a new faculty member is both exciting and overwhelming. It can be very challenging to transition from the role of a graduate student, or in some cases the role of a nonacademic professional, to a faculty position. In making this transition, new faculty are expected to fulfill new responsibilities, understand a new organization, develop relationships with new colleagues, network with key scholars in their area from across the nation and the world, and more.

Several studies have examined the experiences of new faculty, thereby providing insight into factors that could inhibit their success. These studies, summarized by Sorcinelli (1994, p. 474), highlight six areas that contribute to the work stress and career dissatisfaction of new faculty: time constraints in research and teaching; lack of collegial relations; inadequate feedback, recognition, and rewards; unrealistic expectations; insufficient resources; and a lack of balance between work and personal life (figure 4.1).

Mentors play an invaluable role in helping new faculty members manage concerns such as these. They do so, for example, by suggesting strategies for time management, directing new faculty to useful resources (e.g., institutional seed grants and technology support), connecting them to other colleagues, helping them set reasonable goals, and serving as role models. Often a mentor helps with these concerns simply by being a sounding board and constant voice of encouragement. An important role of any mentor is to provide unstinting support and belief in the mentee's abilities and future achievements, even when obstacles or uncertainties arise.

CONTRIBUTORS TO FACULTY SUCCESS

Of course, a mentor's role is not limited to offering support or advice only when problems arise. Mentors also work proactively with their mentees to help them identify and meet their specific career goals (discussed further in chapter 5) and to acquire the many essential competencies needed by any faculty member for success in academe.

---

1. **Time constraints in research and teaching**

   New faculty reported not having enough time to do their work, difficulty juggling teaching and research, and inadequate preparation for teaching. These challenges resulted in the majority reporting health issues such as fatigue, anxiety attacks, and insomnia. Over time faculty reported increased comfort with time management but still reported insufficient time and deteriorating health.

2. **Lack of collegial relations**

   A most disappointing aspect of academe for new faculty was having feelings of isolation, loneliness, and lack of support from colleagues. They desired support in teaching and research, and help in understanding salary and personnel decisions.

3. **Inadequate feedback, recognition, and rewards**

   New faculty members felt their work was "invisible" (without recognition) and were highly anxious about formal evaluations of their performance, especially their teaching evaluations. Over five years their satisfaction with the feedback and recognition they received had increased.

4. **Unrealistic expectations**

   New faculty set very high (often unrealistic) goals for themselves and these were reinforced by supervisors. This resulted in feelings of not measuring up.

5. **Insufficient resources**

   There is a large disparity among new faculty with some receiving excellent resources in their early years (e.g., technicians, research assistants, lab space, secretarial support, funds for pilot studies), but most having great difficulty finding the resources to succeed.

6. **Lack of balance between work and personal life**

   As noted above, new faculty feel a lack of time to do their work. This results in "negative spillover," that is, reduction in the time and energy for nonfaculty responsibilities and leisure.

Figure 4.1.   Contributors to the Work Stress and Career Dissatisfaction of New Faculty
Summary of findings reviewed in "Effective Approaches to New Faculty Development," by M. D. Sorcinelli, 1994, *Journal of Counseling & Development, 72*(5), pp. 474–479.

There are numerous factors, common to all faculty, that are necessary for success in the profession. The factors found to be associated with high academic productivity fall into three domains:

- Characteristics or competencies of the *individual* faculty member,
- Characteristics of the *institution* in which the faculty member works, and
- Characteristics of the *leadership* of that work environment.

These characteristics are defined in figure 4.2, and their interplay is illustrated in figure 4.3. When present and continually fostered, these characteristics help ensure the vitality of faculty and the institutions in which they work.

INDIVIDUAL	INSTITUTIONAL	LEADERSHIP
1. **Socialization:** Understands the values, norms, expectations, and sanctions affecting established faculty (e.g., beneficence, academic freedom).	1. **Recruitment and Selection:** Great effort is expended to recruit and hire members who have the training, goals, commitment, and socialization that match the institution.	1. **Scholar:** Highly regarded as a scholar and educator; serves as a sponsor, mentor, and peer model for other group members.
2. **Motivation:** Driven to explore, understand, and follow one's own ideas through deliberate planning, and to advance and contribute to society through innovation, discovery, and creative works.	2. **Clear Coordinating Goals:** Visible, shared goals coordinate members' work.	2. **Research and Teaching Oriented:** Possesses a "research orientation" and a "teaching orientation"; has internalized the group's research- and education-centered mission.
3. **Content Knowledge:** Familiar —within one's research/ teaching area—with all major published works, projects being conducted, differing theories, key researchers/educators, and predominant funding sources.	3. **Research/Teaching Emphasis:** Research and teaching have appropriate emphasis and are given greater or equal priority than other department goals.	3. **Capably Fulfills All Critical Leadership Roles:** Manager of people and resources
4. **Basic & Advanced Research and Teaching Skills:** Comfortable with statistics, study design, data collection methods, teaching skills, and advanced methods commonly used in one's area.	4. **Culture:** Members are bonded by shared, research-and teaching-related values and practices, have a safe home for testing new ideas.	· Fund raiser · Group advocate · Keeps the group's mission and shared goals visible to all members
5. **Simultaneous Projects:** Engaged in multiple, concurrent projects, so as to buffer against disillusionment if one project stalls or fails.	5. **Positive Group Climate:** The climate is characterized by high morale, dedication to work, low member turnover, and good leader/member relationships.	· Attends to the many individual and institutional features that facilitate research and education productivity and faculty vitality
6. **Orientation:** Committed to both external activities (e.g., regional and national meetings, collaborating with colleagues) and activities within one's own organization (e.g., curriculum planning, institutional governance).	6. **Mentoring:** Beginning and mid-level members are assisted by and collaborate with senior scholars.	4. **Participative Leader:** ∞ Uses an assertive, participative style of leadership
7. **Autonomy & Commitment:** Has academic freedom, plans one's own time and sets one's own goals, but is also committed to and plays a meaningful role within the larger organization.	7. **Communication with Professional Network:** Members have a vibrant network of colleagues with whom they have frequent and substantive (not merely social) research and education communication.	· Holds frequent meetings with clear objectives
8. **Work Habits:** Has established productive scholarly and education habits early on in one's career.	8. **Resources:** Members have access to sufficient resources such as funding, facilities, and especially humans (e.g., local peers for support, research and teaching assistants, technical consultants).	· Creates formal mechanisms and sets expectations for all members to contribute to decision-making[
	9. **Sufficient Work Time:** Members have significant periods of uninterrupted time to devote to work.	· Makes high quality information readily available to the group
	10. **Size/Experience/Expertise:** Members offer different perspectives by virtue of differences in their degree levels, approaches to problems, and varying discipline backgrounds; the group is stable, and its size is at or above a "critical mass."	· Vests ownership of projects with members and values their ideas
	11. **Communication:** Clear and multiple forms of communication so all members feel informed.	
	12. **Rewards:** Research and teaching are rewarded equitably and in accordance with defined benchmarks of achievement; potential rewards include money, promotion, and recognition	
	13. **Brokered Opportunities:** Professional development opportunities are routinely and proactively offered to members to ensure their continued growth and vitality.	
	14. **Decentralized Organization:** Governance structures are flat and decentralized where participation of members is expected.	
	15. **Assertive Participative Governance** Clear and common goals and assertive and participative leadership where active member participation is expected and effective feedback systems are used.	

Figure 4.2. *Individual, Institutional, and Leadership Characteristics That Facilitate Faculty Vitality*
From "A Theoretical, Practical, Predictive Model of Faculty and Department Research Productivity," by C. J. Bland, B. A. Center, D. A. Finstad, K. R. Risbey, and J. G. Staples, 2005, *Academic Medicine, 80*(3), p. 228. Copyright 2005 by Association of American Medical Colleges. Adapted with permission.

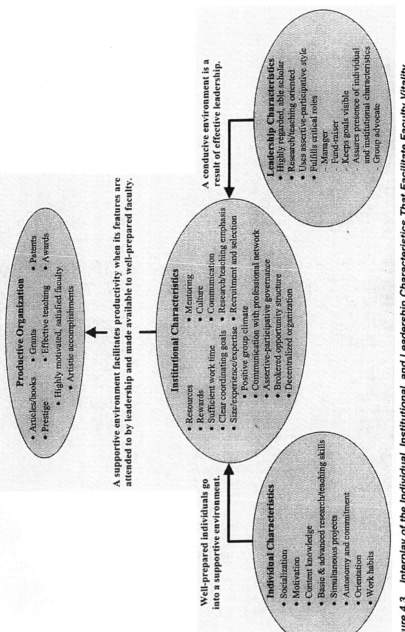

Productive Organization

- Articles/books
- Grants
- Patents
- Prestige
- Effective teaching
- Awards
- Highly motivated, satisfied faculty
- Artistic accomplishments

A supportive environment facilitates productivity when its features are attended to by leadership and made available to well-prepared faculty.

Institutional Characteristics

- Resources
- Mentoring
- Rewards
- Culture
- Sufficient work time
- Communication
- Clear coordinating goals
- Research/teaching emphasis
- Size/experience/expertise
- Recruitment and selection
- Positive group climate
- Communication with professional network
- Assertive-participative governance
- Brokered opportunity structure
- Decentralized organization

A conducive environment is a result of effective leadership.

Leadership Characteristics

- Highly regarded, able scholar
- Research/teaching oriented
- Uses assertive-participative style
- Fulfills critical roles
  - Manager
  - Fund-raiser
  - Keeps goals visible
  - Assures presence of individual and institutional characteristics
  - Group advocate

Well-prepared individuals go into a supportive environment.

Individual Characteristics

- Socialization
- Motivation
- Content knowledge
- Basic & advanced research/teaching skills
- Simultaneous projects
- Autonomy and commitment
- Orientation
- Work habits

Figure 4.3. Interplay of the Individual, Institutional, and Leadership Characteristics That Facilitate Faculty Vitality

From "A Theoretical, Practical, Predictive Model of Faculty and Department Research Productivity," by C. J. Bland, B. A. Center, D. A. Finstad, K. R. Risbey, and J. G. Staples, 2005, *Academic Medicine, 80*(3), p. 227. Copyright 2005 by Association of American Medical Colleges. Adapted with permission.

Most of the research that identified these characteristics used research outcomes as the indicators of productivity or vitality (Bland & Bergquist, 1997; Bland, Center, et al., 2005; Bland, Weber-Main, et al., 2005). Only a small number of studies have assessed faculty vitality through outcomes that measure teacher effectiveness (such as student ratings); however, those that did so found that these same characteristics also made for effective teachers. Moreover, conceptual models for faculty development in all areas, including teacher development, identify similar characteristics. For example, Caffarella and Zinn (1999) cluster the factors that impede or support faculty into four domains: people and interpersonal relationships, institutional structures, personal considerations and commitments, and intellectual and personal characteristics.

In short, a vital and productive institution includes faculty, an institutional environment, and leaders with characteristics such as those described in figures 4.2 and 4.3. Mentors and academic leaders who are knowledgeable about the full range of these success-facilitating characteristics are advantaged in their role. They can take steps to assess which characteristics are missing or weak in their mentees' background and environments, then identify strategies to fill in these gaps. More details about these characteristics and some examples of how mentors and academic leaders can positively influence them are provided next.

Institutional and Leadership Characteristics for Faculty Vitality

Leaders in higher education understand the need to hire, continually develop, and retain the best faculty. Yet, no matter how well prepared a faculty member is, he or she is not likely to thrive if placed in an ill-suited environment. In fact, the literature finds that environmental features are the most powerful predictors of an academic's productivity (Blackburn, 1979; Bland, Hitchcock, Anderson, & Stritter, 1987; Bland et al., 2002; Clark & Lewis, 1985; Dundar & Lewis, 1998; Long & McGinnis, 1981; McGee & Ford, 1987; Pellino, Boberg, Blackburn, & O'Connell, 1981; Perkoff, 1985; Perry, Clifton, Menec, Struthers, & Menges, 2000; Teodorescu, 2000).

Important features of the academic environment include such things as sufficient resources, stimulating colleagues, adequate work time, and high-quality mentoring. Important leadership characteristics include having a leader who uses a participative approach to governance and keeps the goals of the unit visible to the members. Notably, "[it] is the leader who heavily influences the presence or absence of all other institutional characteristics—from setting clear goals and maintaining a research [and/or education] emphasis within the group, to developing fair, effective reward systems and allocating funds for needed technical resources" (Bland, Weber-Main, et al., 2005, p. 190).

With regard to leadership, the influence of a department head on new faculty can be significant. Sorcinelli (1988, 1992) and Turner and Boice (1987) found that new faculty identified their chairperson as a crucial advocate and, in some cases, the most important individual during their first year. Chairs who were cited as particularly helpful took time to assign courses that fit interests and priorities, to negotiate minimal preps or a reduced load, to secure internal funds for resources or travel, and to provide guidance for annual review. Conversely, chairs who assigned excessive workloads and provided little mentoring to new faculty were a dominant source of stress. In large departments, it is likely the division head or program director who would have the impact of the department chair described above.

For all of these reasons, it is critical that the mentors of new faculty understand not only the mentee's background and training, but also the environment in which he or she is operating. Armed with a detailed understanding of the mentee's work setting and its leadership, a mentor can look for ways to affirm or facilitate a positive environment for the mentee. For example, mentors can advise new faculty on how to develop a productive relationship with their department head and other influential local leaders, access a wide variety of institutional resources, or negotiate for reduced course loads.

In turn, academic leaders have a responsibility to understand, first and foremost, the tremendous influence that institutional features have on the vitality of individual faculty members. Moreover, leaders must understand the degree to which they themselves are responsible for ensuring the presence and preservation of all the institutional features that characterize a productive organization, including mentoring. To this end, suggestions for supporting mentoring via a formal mentoring program were provided in chapter 3, and additional mentoring principles and tools are provided throughout this book. Suggested strategies for initiating and maintaining the many *other* essential characteristics of productive organizations have been identified from qualitative research on highly research-productive departments and schools (Bland, Weber-Main, et al., 2005).

Individual Characteristics (Essential Competencies) for Faculty Vitality

All new faculty members arrive in their profession with at least one essential individual competency already established: advanced knowledge in their discipline. However, content knowledge is only one of many competencies needed for advancement in the profession. Faculty are also expected to grow in a large number of educational, research, communication, administrative, and academic professional areas. Examples of specific competencies in these areas are outlined in figure 4.4. By acquiring all of the competencies mastered by successful faculty, new faculty are more likely to readily overcome obstacles, achieve their goals, and embark on a highly productive, satisfying career.

Certainly, new faculty will enter their profession having already acquired many of these competencies during their previous training or work experience. For example, a new faculty member with a previous career as a high school teacher will have many of the education competencies. A new faculty member who previously served as a researcher at the National Institutes of Health will have many of the research competencies. However, the presence and depth of these competencies cannot be assumed. Further, even faculty who enter the profession with strength in most of these competencies may need help applying them in a new institutional setting and in their new role.

Mentors have a responsibility to facilitate mentees' acquisition of the essential competencies, particularly in areas in which the new faculty member has less experience. For example, in the research area, mentors might review the mentee's manuscripts before submission to journals, participate in peer reviews of the mentee's grant proposals, offer access to a talented statistical consultant, or help identify potential funding sources in the mentee's research area. In the education area, mentors might team-teach with the mentee, share lecture notes, or observe and provide feedback on teaching. To facilitate administration competencies,

Professional Academic Competencies
∞ Effectively manage productive career in academia
∞ Understand values, ethics, behavior codes of academia
∞ Establish & maintain network of professional colleagues

Education Competencies
∞ Design curricula
∞ Develop courses, presentations, course materials
∞ Instruct small and large groups in different educational settings, including on-line
∞ Assess student performance
∞ Evaluate program effectiveness

Research Competencies
∞ Use range of information-searching tools
∞ Synthesize theory and empirical findings in a research area and relate to one's own research.
∞ Formulate a research question, operationalize variables
∞ Design descriptive and/or explanatory studies
∞ Collect and analyze data
∞ Use design and statistical consultants
∞ Evaluate and discuss study findings, strengths, limitations
∞ Conduct and manage research projects in an ethical manner
∞ Locate appropriate funding sources

Communication Competencies
∞ Prepare clear written documents
∞ Speak clearly
∞ Use computer technologies for communication, education, research, and administration

Administration Competencies
∞ Understand impact of trends (economic, social, political) on academic life
∞ Understand academic organizational structures and their relationships
∞ Provide leadership for small and large group academic tasks

Figure 4.4.   Illustrative List of Essential Faculty Competencies
From *Successful Faculty in Academic Medicine: Essential Skills and How to Acquire Them* (pp. 22–23), by C. J. Bland, C. C. Schmitz, F. T. Stritter, R. C. Henry, and J. A. Aluise, 1990, New York: Springer Publishing. Copyright 2007 by Carole J. Bland. Adapted with permission.

mentors might nominate the mentee for an appropriate leadership position or recommend a workshop on effective management.

These are all important ways of facilitating mentees' careers. Highly motivated new faculty, however, can acquire many of the advanced teaching, research, and administrative skills on their own. In contrast, the professional academic competencies, which include learning the unwritten rules and practices of a new profession, are best developed with the help of an experienced, successful colleague. These competencies are not typically acquired through formal instruction, but through a process called socialization. Thus, we devote much of the remainder of this chapter to the important role mentors play in the socialization of new faculty members.

SOCIALIZATION: A MECHANISM FOR ACQUIRING PROFESSIONAL ACADEMIC COMPETENCIES

Successful faculty have a set of professional academic competencies that are typically acquired via a process called socialization (Bland et al., 1990). "Socialization is a mechanism through which new members learn the values, norms, knowledge, beliefs, and the interpersonal and other skills that facilitate role performance and further group goals" (Mortimer & Simmons, 1978, p. 423).

In addition to facilitating effective performance, socialization is the means for "developing commitment to work, for stimulating motivation, and for internalizing occupationally relevant attitudes and behaviors that sustain productivity and continued achievement throughout the career" (Clark & Corcoran, 1986, p. 23). This second outcome of socialization is especially important for professional academics and the organizations that employ them, given that faculty typically stay in their profession for a lifetime.

A great deal has been written about the importance of socialization as a mechanism to acquire essential skills for success. Researchers in this area have been particularly interested in socialization to professions and organizations (e.g., Bucher & Stelling, 1977; Dubin, 1976; Mortimer & Simmons, 1978; Nyre & Reilly, 1979; Van Maanen & Schein, 1979), and specifically the career development of exceptionally productive faculty (Aran & Ben-David, 1968; Bland & Schmitz, 1986; Corcoran & Clark, 1984; Creswell, 1986; Pelz & Andrews, 1966). Virtually all of these studies conclude that socialization is critical for effective performance in a profession and in an organization. Conway and Glass (1978), in "Socialization for Survival in the Academic World," state, "If the faculty of a given school wish to see that school ranked among the acknowledged best in the university, the socialization of each new faculty member must become a concern of the corporate body" (p. 429).

"Let me show you the ropes."

This alone suggests that socialization is an activity to which mentoring should attend.

Creswell (1986), in his extensive review of 130 studies on faculty research productivity, found socialization to be a fundamental career event in predicting scientific productivity. In study after study, socialization factors were the critical feature that eventually differentiated highly productive from less productive faculty. In most of these studies, productivity was measured by publications. Even in studies where "highly productive" is defined more broadly, successful socialization appears to predict which faculty members will be high achievers and which will not.

All professions, not just faculty in higher education, are character-ized by a unique set of unwritten norms, rules, and practices. Effective attorneys, scientists, priests, and physicians, for example, know more than law, science, religion, or medicine. They have learned many un-written rules, concepts, and behaviors that allow them to "act like an at-torney" or "think like a scientist." They have acquired the professional attitudes and social skills of their chosen occupation. These skills include a "somewhat special language, an ideology that helps edit a member's everyday experience, shared standards of relevance as to the critical aspects of the work that is being accomplished, matter-of-fact prejudices, models for social etiquette and demeanor, certain customs and rituals suggestive of how members are to relate to colleagues, sub-ordinates, superiors, and outsiders . . ." (Van Maanen & Schein, 1979, p. 210).

Mentors might be inclined to neglect socialization to academe for mentees who have previously been socialized to another profession and who have significant life experience. This might include architects, public school administrators, business executives, lawyers, physicians, and other professionals. Still, it is important for these faculty to un-derstand where their first socialization applies to higher education and where it does not. Professional values and practices can differ. For ex-ample, trial attorneys value adversarial strategies for identifying truth, whereas scientists value collaborative approaches. It is also important for these faculty to understand the core values, unwritten rules, and common practices of the academic profession and/or the university system—in sum, acquire a second socialization. For example, a core value of academe that may not be familiar to faculty members coming from another profession is academic freedom. Similarly, they would likely not be familiar with the regulations or best practices for the pro-tection of human subjects in research.

PROFESSIONAL ACADEMIC COMPETENCIES: DEFINITIONS AND MENTORING RESPONSIBILITIES

Having described the importance of socialization, we now focus more in depth on the specific professional academic competencies that need to be acquired through the socialization process. For faculty, the professional academic competencies can be clustered into three categories: career management skills, academic values, and professional academic networks. Having these abilities enhances a faculty member's sense of competence, identity as an academic, and career advancement.

Effectively Manage Career

For some faculty, a career just happens and is advanced—or not— by the serendipitous events that come along. Most successful faculty, however, did not succeed purely by chance, but rather were proactive in managing their careers. A mentor can play a very important role in helping a mentee with career management in terms of goal articulation and understanding the organization.

Knowledge about one's organization—its structure, governance, rewards, career paths, key players, and so forth—is essential for successful participation (Bogdewic, 1986; Dill, 1986). For the academic this means knowing about the institution's mission, administrative structure, and promotion procedure. Because faculty are affected by factors outside their local institutions, their success is also determined by their knowledge of external organizations, such as funding organizations, professional organizations, and academic and educational organizations.

In most nonacademic organizations, promotion mechanisms controlled by others advance personnel either automatically (e.g., according to seniority) or selectively (e.g., through invitation to join a medical group or become a partner in a law firm). In academic settings, however, individual faculty members are personally responsible for understanding how to advance in the organization. Faculty are expected to understand all levels of their organization and how to play a role in it; to be aware of the time frame and criteria for advancement; to identify and satisfy advancement criteria; to manage their work flow to accommodate professional advancement tasks; to maintain a dossier documenting how they meet the criteria; and to propose themselves for review and promotion at appropriate times. Occasionally there is help with these various steps along the way. For example, a department head may establish a yearly "contract" with faculty members to guide time management, or a department may provide assistance in preparing a promotion packet. If a faculty member does not advance, however, it is seldom considered the institution's problem; rather, the faculty member is considered at fault. Career management is clearly the faculty member's responsibility.

In summary, faculty members need to understand how their institution and related organizations influence their career. At the same time, faculty need to establish their own career-related goals, including what is expected of them by others. In short, faculty need to know how to effectively manage a productive career in academe. Thus, it is important that mentors help faculty do the following:

- Describe their own career vision, goals, strategies for accomplishing goals, and timeline for goals. Chapter 5 provides guidance on how to do this.
- Understand the purpose, goals, structure, governance, and key players in their organization (e.g., department, college, hospital, or university).
- Assess how well the organization's goals and expectations match with their career vision, desired skills, interests, activities, and goals.
- Understand the daily activities of successful academics (e.g., develop, administer, and teach courses; read broadly in areas affecting their discipline and institution; conduct research; participate in local, institutional, and national committees and review panels; work in multiple sites such as experiment station, office, clinic, hospital, or on the road).
- Understand the activities and products that lead to promotion and rewards.
- Identify relevant journals and understand how to publish in them.
- Understand major funding sources, professional organizations, and academic organizations.

Understand Academic Values

Understanding the values, norms, and traditions of the profession and organization in which one works is critical. It is these elements, rather than shared technical knowledge alone, that bond a group to a profession and allow them to work together effectively. Given a common understanding and view of the world, professionals can overcome knowledge differences and agree on goals and means to an end.

According to Blackburn and Fox's (1976) study of medical faculty, Caffrey's (1969) study of liberal arts schools, and other writers in this area (e.g., Rice, 1983), the highly ranked norms of academics are academic freedom and the priority of research and excellence in teaching.

The importance of professional values is not to be underestimated. In addition to providing a basis for efficient work, they communicate basic philosophical beliefs held by people in the profession. Academics, for example, hold common beliefs about preferred methods of establishing the truth or explaining phenomena. Knowing the underlying values allows a faculty member to understand why persons in the profession behave as they do, to predict a professional's behavior, and to know how to behave in accordance with others in that profession. Understanding academic values allows faculty to apply their skills and direct their activities more effectively. Such understanding also enables faculty to defuse value conflicts.

Unfortunately, studies suggest that new faculty are no longer sensing a common set of values in their organization (e.g., Sorcinelli, 1994). They are frequently being placed in a variety of appointment types with differing expectations, working in remote, isolated settings, and having less contact with senior faculty (Rice, Sorcinelli, Dean, & Austin, 2000). Many senior faculty, too, are reporting a loss of esprit de corps in their departments (Bland & Bergquist, 1997). Thus, departments must be proactive in establishing mechanisms to be sure that the expectations in different tracks are understood and appreciated, to socialize new faculty, and to maintain a culture.

In summary, faculty need to understand the underlying values, traditions, and unwritten behavior codes of academe. Thus, it is important that mentors help faculty do the following:

- Understand the values of academics (e.g., academic freedom, ethical standards, importance of knowledge production, research subject protection, publishing, student growth and development, patient care and safety).

- Understand how these values do or do not permeate policies and missions of the institution (e.g., regent's mission statement, promotion and tenure code, grievance process, institutional review board procedures, required Responsible Conduct of Research training, dean's priorities for the school, priorities of the university, university senate policies on such things as conflict of interest and academic code of conduct).
- Identify unwritten rules and practices of academics (e.g., authorship on articles, establishing collaborative research relationships, soliciting information from potential funding sources, partnering with other organizations).
- Ascertain how well one's own values match with academic and institutional values.
- Identify (and adapt to, when appropriate) different value systems within the department, university, professional societies, practicing community, and funding agencies (e.g., private foundations, National Institutes of Health, National Science Foundation).
- Understand the rules and policies of academic conduct in research and teaching.

Establish and Maintain Professional Academic Networks

In academe, the nature of faculty work is, paradoxically, both independent and dependent. For instance, a researcher conducts his or her daily routine quite autonomously, either alone or with a small team. At the same time, the researcher is very dependent on the previous work of others to build on and advance the body of knowledge. Whether reporting results of research, teaching, or new management techniques, all authors are dependent on others to critique and replicate their work and to maintain the quality of work in the field through grant reviews, refereed journals, conference presentations, and critiques. Because of this interdependence, successful academics have a network of professional colleagues who are vital to their effective performance. These colleagues are usually peers, superiors, or former mentors. They may be located at the same or other institutions. They do such things as provide quick access to the most recent work in the area, serve as "thinking partners" when the researcher is stumped, and open doors to peer review panels.

Numerous studies have found a positive correlation between a vital network of colleagues and faculty success. In fact, having such a network is a major predictor of research productivity (Aran & Ben-David, 1968; Blackburn, 1979; Bland & Ruffin, IV, 1992; Bland & Schmitz, 1986; Blau, 1976; Corcoran & Clark, 1984; Fox, 1991; Kelly, 1986; Pelz & Andrews, 1966; Sindermann, 1985; Tschannen-Moran, Firestone, Hoy, & Johnson, 2000; Visart, 1979). A cross-national study by Teodorescu (2000) found that "membership in professional societies and attendance of professional conferences was a significant correlate of article productivity in all the countries in the sample" (p. 216). Indeed, attending—or more ideally presenting at—scholarly conferences is one of the most important means by which faculty develop their research networks. Similarly, Bearinger stated, "The only way to get national recognition is to pump out research and publish and then present it at national meetings. It's very hard to have a national reputation if you don't show up at meetings, meet people, and get involved" (Bland, Weber-Main, et al., 2005, p. 103).

It is also important to communicate regularly between conferences with other faculty in one's network. In their study of ten thousand scientists in twelve hundred different research groups in six countries, Pelz and Andrews (1966) found that the most productive researchers had the most frequent conversations with colleagues (e.g., fifteen hours a week) and spent the most time doing such things as reviewing drafts of colleagues' papers, visiting one another's labs, and exchanging reprints. In their review of professional academic networks, Hitchcock, Bland, Hekelman, and Blumenthal (1995) concluded that faculty who communicate more with colleagues produce more and better research, are promoted more quickly, are more likely to receive an increase in income and to be the recipients of distinguished awards, and report a higher satisfaction with the work itself. Networks also facilitate teaching success, as they provide like-minded colleagues with whom to discuss curriculum ideas and share teaching materials and strategies.

Given how essential a professional network is to faculty success, it is often an area on which mentors focus. On the basis of his study of successful researchers, Blackburn (1979) wrote: "Mentorship/sponsorship in the first years is critical for launching a productive career—Learning the informal network that supports productivity—the inner workings of professional associations and who the productive people are, for example is critical, especially in the faculty member's first years" (pp. 25–26). Similarly, Aran and Ben-David (1968) found that medical researchers attached "great importance to their continued contact with the scientists whom they had met during their resocialization. . . . [and] that change in productivity following resocialization is indeed a function of the intensity of communication of the researcher with other scientists, i.e., of his [or her] induction into the scientific community" (pp. 12–13).

In summary, faculty need to be able to establish, maintain, and communicate with a network of professional colleagues in academe. Thus, it is important that mentors help faculty do the following:

- Maintain productive (versus social) professional relationships with an advisor or mentor(s) and with peers.
- Maintain frequent, substantive contact with productive researchers in one's research and education areas, both within one's institution and elsewhere.
- Seek opportunities to collaborate (e.g., combine resources, personnel, activities, and goals) across one's network.
- Participate in professional groups and activities associated with the college, hospital, university, discipline, research and teaching areas, or funding sources.
- Build contacts with funding sources and maintain relationships with project officers and educational experts.

SUMMARY

Mentors are responsible for helping mentees develop the abilities they need to lead a successful and satisfying career as faculty. Mentors do this in two ways: by helping mentees achieve their own unique career objectives and by helping mentees acquire essential competencies for success in academe. Particularly important is the socialization process whereby mentees learn how to successfully manage their career, learn about and internalize academic values, and establish and maintain a vital professional network. By acquiring these professional academic competencies, the new faculty member is positioned to avoid many of the typical areas of concern for new faculty that were described in the beginning of this chapter.

Now the question becomes, exactly how does mentoring result in these desired outcomes? How does it really work? We answer these questions in the next chapter, in which we describe how the mentoring process proceeds and provide guidance for accomplishing each step in the process.

CHAPTER 5

Phases of Effective Mentoring

Chapter Highlights

- *Mentoring is a dynamic interaction that passes through defined phases. In the preparing and negotiating phases, the mentor and mentee assess the suitability of the match and lay the foundation for a good working relationship. The mentor and mentee then establish a mentoring agreement. The agreement includes ground rules for working together and specific steps, with a timeline, for achieving the mentee's career vision.*

- *Clarifying a career vision and mission is one of the most important initial career development steps for a new faculty member. Using the vision and mission as targets, the mentee and mentor can more readily set strategic goals and annual objectives that, if successfully met, will bring the mentee closer to his or her vision.*

- *In the enabling phase, mentoring strategies such as role modeling, advising, advocacy, reviewing, and collaboration are used to help the mentee achieve his or her goals and objectives. This continues until goals are achieved, new goals are set, or a mutual decision is made to end the mentoring relationship (the closing phase).*

- *Mentors and mentees alike have a responsibility to keep the relationship vital and moving forward. Mentors provide support, challenge, and vision. Mentees understand their role, commit to a work plan, and use "mentee skills," such as asking productive questions and internalizing their mentor's input.*

INTRODUCTION

When we defined faculty mentoring in the beginning of this book, we emphasized that mentoring is a professional relationship that develops over time, passing through a series of phases. As Ritchie and Genoni (2002) aptly noted, "There is more than just a short-term or passing interest on the part of the mentor" and the mentee (p. 69).

In this chapter we describe the process of mentoring as it occurs over the life span of the relationship. Although each mentoring relationship is unique, there are common stages that characterize the mentoring process (Daloz, 1999; Rolfe, 2006; Wanberg et al., 2003; Zachary, 2000). It is within these stages that mentors and mentees are matched, the mentee's specific needs and goals are assessed, objectives are defined, commitments are made, strategies are put forth, tasks are assigned, and progress is evaluated. Ultimately, the decision is made to end the relationship or continue it. In the latter case, new goals are articulated to guide the mentee's continued career development.

In describing how these many elements of faculty mentoring proceed, we have drawn largely from Zachary's (2000) description of the four phases of effective mentoring:

1. Preparing Phase: The mentor and mentee learn about each other and prepare for their roles. The suitability of the match is assessed, and a decision is made to proceed (or not) to the next phase.
2. Negotiating Phase: The mentor and mentee learn more about each other and use this information to establish specific goals, activities, and responsibilities. Ways of working together are defined (time and frequency of meetings, issues of confidentiality, and boundary setting). The results of this stage set the foundation for building trust and establishing what is to be accomplished, how, and by when.
3. Enabling Phase: The mentor and mentee have the most contact during this phase. Mentee growth is facilitated through strategies such as collaborations, sponsorship, training, support, challenge, and more.
4. Closing Phase: After a mentee has accomplished the defined mentoring goals, the mentoring relationship ends or new goals are established and a new mentoring relationship is negotiated.

We next describe each of these phases in more detail as they apply to the mentoring of higher education faculty. For simplicity, our description of the four phases of mentoring is oriented to a traditional mentoring relationship, in which a senior faculty member(s) is mentoring a junior faculty member. However, it is important to remember that these phases will occur in some way regardless of the mentoring model used or the career stage of the faculty mentee. In chapter 8, we provide examples of how the different mentoring phases apply to midcareer and senior faculty being mentored through a peer or group approach. In chapter 9, we apply the mentoring phases to faculty who seek to assume an administrative leadership role.

PREPARING PHASE

Make the Match

The first step in a mentoring relationship is the matching of mentors and mentees. In a formal mentoring program, this step is usually initiated by the organization. Mentor selection can occur in a variety of ways. Bland, Weber-Main, and colleagues (2005) found that within highly research-productive departments at the University of Minnesota, matching strategies were tailored according to the size, diversity, and geographic proximity of their faculty. In all cases the mentee and mentor were consulted before the final matching was done. Some illustrative examples from this study—drawn from different disciplines and readily applicable to other institutions—are as follows:

- In one department, two senior faculty members are assigned to each new faculty member. One mentor has research interests that are closely aligned with the new faculty member's content area. The second mentor is drawn from outside the area. This strategy is thought to facilitate cross-pollination of ideas and interdisciplinary work.
- In several departments and schools, new tenure-track faculty are assigned to one or more senior mentors to specifically support and monitor the mentees' progress toward promotion.
- In another department, new faculty members are expected to interview each senior faculty member in the department. He or she

then meets with the department head to agree upon a mentor. The end result is a traditional "one mentor-one mentee" model, but the matching process involves both the mentee and the department head.

- In some smaller departments, the department head serves as the mentor for all new faculty.
- One division's mentoring program directly connects faculty with senior mentors from other departments. The intent is to allow new faculty to talk candidly with senior people who understand the larger institution's promotion and tenure system, but who will not be directly voting for or against promotion of the mentee.

Assess the Fit

Mentors and mentees alike should take the time to assess early on, as well as possible, whether a particular mentoring arrangement is right. Even for experienced mentors, it is important to reflect on the match before accepting the commitment.

Assessing the fit takes place through a series of conversations and other types of information exchanges between the mentor and mentee. Potential mentors can use these exchanges to learn about the predominant needs and goals of the mentee, as well as get a general sense of their compatibility as colleagues. Similarly, mentees need to learn about the potential mentor's background, with the aim of assessing whether this person has the experience, access to opportunities, and time to help the mentee meet his or her goals. Mentees may find it helpful to review the mentor's vita and publications, talk with former mentees, and discuss the mentor's qualifications with other trusted colleagues.

Figure 5.1 is a checklist of items that mentors and mentees should ask themselves during the preparing phase. These items reflect several important aspects of mentoring that need to be present for the relationship to succeed: sincere and mutual interest and compatibility, shared assumptions about the mentoring process and roles, enthusiasm to offer/accept help, sufficient time to commit to the relationship, and a willingness to develop new skills.

All parties in a faculty mentoring relationship should remember that mentoring has a defined purpose: to help faculty acquire the key

Instructions: Complete the following checklist to determine if you have sufficiently completed the preparing phase.

Mentor items	**Mentee items**
___ 1. I have a sincere interest in helping this person succeed.	___ 1. I have a sincere interest in having this person as a mentor.
___ 2. There appears to be mutual interest and compatibility.	___ 2. There appears to be mutual interest and compatibility.
___ 3. Our assumptions about the process are congruent.	___ 3. Our assumptions about the process are congruent.
___ 4. I am clear about my role.	___ 4. I am clear about my role.
___ 5. I am the right person to help the mentee achieve his or her goals.	___ 5. This person is the right mentor to help me achieve my goals.
___ 6. I can enthusiastically engage in helping this person.	___ 6. I can enthusiastically engage in being mentored by this person.
___ 7. I am willing to use my network of contacts to help this individual.	___ 7. I am ready to accept help from this mentor's network of contacts.
___ 8. I can commit adequate time to mentoring this person.	___ 8. I can commit adequate time to being mentored by this person.
___ 9. I have access to the kind of opportunities that can support this person's learning.	___ 9. This person has access to the kind of opportunities that can support my learning.
___ 10. I have the support that I need to be able to engage in this relationship in a meaningful way.	___ 10. I am ready and able to engage in this relationship in a meaningful way.
___ 11. I am committed to developing my own mentoring skills.	___ 11. I am committed to using this relationship to help develop my skills and meet my goals.

Figure 5.1.   Checklist for the Preparing Phase of Mentoring
Mentor items are from *The Mentor's Guide: Facilitating Effective Learning Relationships* (p. 92), by L. J. Zachary, 2000, San Francisco: Jossey-Bass. Copyright 2000 by Jossey-Bass Inc. Adapted with permission of John Wiley & Sons, Inc.

competencies and constructive work relationships they need to lead successful and satisfying careers in academe. Thus, although both mentor and mentee must be sincerely interested in working with each other, their personalities and perspectives can differ. The key question to answer is whether or not this mentor (or team of mentors) is the most appropriate advisor for this mentee, at this time, considering the faculty member's current development needs and long-term professional aspirations. It is during the next phase (negotiating) that these needs and aspirations are articulated in more detail.

NEGOTIATING PHASE

If the mentor and mentee decide they are a likely match (on the basis of their initial conversations, self-reflection, and background review), then the next step is negotiation. In the negotiating phase, the mentor and mentee accomplish three things. First, they lay the groundwork for the mentoring activities to come by learning more about each other. In this regard, the preparing and negotiating phases often occur simultaneously, especially when the mentor has had little or no experience with the potential mentee. Second, the mentor and mentee create ground rules for working together (time and frequency of meetings, issues of confidentiality, and boundary setting). Third, using information acquired during the previous series of information exchanges, the mentee and mentor establish a clear mentoring plan that articulates all of the following: the mentee's career vision, mission, goals, annual objectives, strategies, and timeline. The final outcome of the negotiating phase is a mentoring agreement, in which all aspects of the mentoring plan and the relationship ground rules are clearly defined.

Lay the Foundation

Once the mentor and mentee have decided to work together, there is usually a need for more in-depth sharing of background information. In their first meeting, the mentor might ask questions to understand better the mentee's training, experience, professional strengths and weaknesses, current and past positions, and career aspirations. In chapter 4 we summarized the many individual, environmental, and leadership characteristics that the literature consistently finds present in a vital academic institution. The mentor could ask the mentee to complete self-assessments in each of these areas. (We provide these assessment tools as Appendices B and C.) The results can be reviewed together as a means of identifying specific objectives for inclusion in the mentoring plan, described below.

As part of laying the foundation, the mentor also shares more about his or her background, accomplishments, and career vision. This provides the mentee with insights into the mentor's career (beyond those gathered in the preparing phase) and highlights specific ways the mentor can be of assistance. It is unlikely that one mentor will meet all of a mentee's needs. More likely, multiple mentors will be more effective. Some departments routinely establish mentoring teams for new faculty from the start. In any case, honest discussions during the negotiating phase will make it easier for a mentor to identify when it is in the best interests of the mentee to refer to other resources or bring in an additional mentoring partner.

These conversations also facilitate the establishment of an open, collegial relationship between the mentor and mentee. Writers on mentoring stress the importance of building an open relationship from the beginning, so as to provide a positive climate for mentee learning. Daloz (1999) makes this point eloquently: "Trust is the well from which we draw the courage to let go of what we no longer need and to receive what we do. Without a reasonably well-established sense of basic trust, it is difficult to move ahead" (p. 206). We discuss the topic of establishing trust and other strategies for establishing effective mentoring relationships in chapter 6.

Create the Ground Rules

An important part of any mentoring relationship is a clear set of mutually agreed upon ground rules. The ground rules include such things as when and where meetings will occur, the expectations for completing agreed upon assignments, and the kind of access the mentee has to the mentor (whether appointments are needed or the mentee needs to go through a gatekeeper). All of these details should be decided early on, during the negotiating phase. It is particularly important for the mentor and mentee to agree on confidentiality assumptions. Figure 5.2 is a checklist of assumptions about confidentiality that should be carefully discussed and, perhaps, even included in the final mentoring agreement.

Instructions: Answer each question with "yes," "no," or "not sure." Make copies of this checklist before you complete it. Complete a copy yourself, and ask your mentee to complete a copy. When you have completed all eight items, decide whether there are other assumptions that you hold that should be added to the list. Review and discuss each item with your mentee. Allow for a full discussion of gaps before coming to consensus.

Which of the following assumptions about confidentiality do you hold?

____ 1. What we discuss stays between us.

____ 2. If asked by your supervisor, I can freely disclose our conversation.

____ 3. After our formal mentoring relationship has ended, it is okay to talk about what we discussed or how we related.

____ 4. If there is a demonstrated need to know, I can appropriately disclose our conversations, my impressions, or anything else that pertains to the relationship.

____ 5. What we say between us stays there unless you give me permission to talk about it with others.

____ 6. Some issues will be kept confidential, while others will not.

____ 7. It is okay to discuss how we relate to one another but not the content of our discussions.

____ 8. It is okay to talk about what we talk about as long as it is positive.

Are there other assumptions I hold that should be added to this list?

Figure 5.2. Checklist for Assumption Testing About Confidentiality
From *The Mentor's Guide: Facilitating Effective Learning Relationships* (p. 105), by L. J. Zachary, 2000, San Francisco: Jossey-Bass. Copyright 2000 by Jossey-Bass Inc. Adapted with permission of John Wiley & Sons, Inc.

Establish the Mentoring Plan

At this point in the mentoring relationship, background information has been exchanged, the decision to proceed with the mentoring arrangement has been affirmed, and ground rules have been set. The next step is to establish the mentoring plan. This step is critical. An effective mentoring plan delineates clear expectations for what will be accomplished via mentoring. On the whole, the mentoring plan defines the impact that a mentee wants to make through his or her work (i.e., a career vision), then outlines a logical plan for making that vision a reality.

To create a mentoring plan, it is helpful to think of a continuum of career planning. At one end of the continuum is the mentee's career

Figure 5.3. Charting Your Course to Achieve Your Vision

vision, and at the other end are the mentee's annual work plans. In between are two additional key points in the continuum, the career mission and strategic goals. Figure 5.3 displays how these parts of the career plan work together to help faculty chart a course for their career. The final "destination" is the faculty member's career vision. Having a career plan (chart) helps the mentee stay on course and navigate effectively toward his or her vision.

We define each of these four career-planning steps next, working backward from the vision and mission and drilling down to the more detailed and readily measurable strategic goals and annual objectives.

- *Step 1: State a career vision.* A career vision statement describes what the world looks and feels like as a result of the mentee doing his or her work. A vision statement answers the question, "*What does the mentee want to be a part of creating?*"

A compelling and crystal clear vision statement can have a magnetic effect, pulling the mentee toward it as he or she focuses on the vision.

A new physician researcher might express her vision as a world without Alzheimer's disease. A new faculty member in education might articulate his career vision as a world without gaps in the academic performance among high school students of different races.

Stating one's career vision, particularly for the first time, requires reflection. The mentee should think about what drives him or her as a faculty member. What is his or her burning passion? In a study of medical school faculty, passion for one's work was the characteristic that best predicted faculty productivity (Bland, Center, et al., 2005). This is a consistent finding in studies on highly successful faculty, along with the finding that these faculty have systematic strategies for addressing this passion (Bland et al., 2002). Once the vision is articulated, the mentee and mentor can take this vision and move it closer to action plans by articulating a career mission and goals.

- *Step 2: State a career mission.* A career mission defines what the mentee will do in order to achieve his or her vision. A mission statement answers the question, *"How* will the mentee do his or her part to achieve the vision?"

The mission is the reason why the mentee works at this particular job or in this particular institution in the first place. It is what gives meaning to the mentee's work and academic life. The mission for the aforementioned education faculty member might be to conduct research to identify the causes of student achievement gaps. For years, the mission of AT&T was: "We are dedicated to being the world's best at bringing people together—giving them easy access to each other and to the information and services they want and need—anytime."

- *Step 3: State strategic goals.* Strategic goals are statements describing what the mentee wants to accomplish in the years ahead in order to achieve his or her career mission and vision. A strategic goal is both achievable and measurable.

Goals are the targets at which the mentee aims. They are articulated in such a straightforward way that an objective third party can tell whether the goal has been achieved. Mentors can, and should, assist

"I WAS LOOKING FOR A LITTLE STRONGER MISSION STATEMENT THAN THAT."

© Dave Carpenter from www.CartoonStock.com

the mentee in developing goals for the upcoming year(s). One way a mentor can do this is to ask the mentee to "think back from the future." That is, ten years from now or five years from now, what will the mentee have accomplished that will have enabled him or her to get closer to achieving his or her mission? A ten-year strategic goal for our example education faculty member might be to establish a multidisciplinary center for the study of high school student academic achievement.

When working with mentees to develop their career vision, mission, and goals, mentors must also provide feedback on how these match with their institution's vision, mission, and goals. If the mentees' plans and those of their department and college are not congruent, it is unlikely that mentees will be able to achieve their dream in their current organization. Academic leaders have a responsibility to ensure that

Dwight D. Eisenhower, 34th U.S. president

In 1943, General Dwight D. Eisenhower took command of the Allied forces in World War II. He was given the following mission: "Proceed to London. Invade Europe. Defeat the Germans." From this mission he generated many strategic goals and plans to get his troops to London, with supplies and proper training to invade Europe. But this was not his vision. His vision was a world without war, without hate, where people were free to choose their governance.

Having a clear mission served General Eisenhower well, helping him to stay the course through multiple strategic plans. The power of his vision is even more compelling. It provided him an enduring dream that guided his next goal—to be president of the United States. Without knowing his vision, these two goals might seem inconsistent. In fact, both were ideal goals for making the impact on the world that he envisioned through his career.

Image courtesy of the Ollie Atkins Collection, Special Collections & Archives, George Mason University Libraries.

institutional goals are clearly and routinely communicated to faculty, particular those who will be serving as mentors to new faculty. Within the context of a mentoring program, this communication might be achieved through mentor-mentee training sessions led by high-level administrators. As described in chapter 3, the goals and culture of the larger organization should be reflected in the goals of any institutionally supported mentoring program.

- *Step 4: State annual objectives, with timelines and outcomes.* Annual objectives are the concrete outcomes the mentee expects to accomplish as a result of the next year's work.

Typically, annual objectives are part of an annual plan that delineates the activities a mentee will do and the outcomes he or she will achieve over the next twelve months. Outcomes can include such things as acquire a grant, submit three journal articles, revise one course, learn a new procedure, or produce a certain amount of clinical income. Often, these plans have a timeline noting target dates for completion of each objective. If the mentee writes these plans in the context of his or her mission, vision, and goals for the next five to ten years, it will ensure that each year's accomplishments will bring the mentee closer to achieving his or her vision.

Over time it is likely that some of the mentee's annual objectives will relate to specific skills he or she needs to acquire in order to achieve a strategic goal and the career mission. For example, if the education faculty member in our example above is going to establish a multidisciplinary research center, this person will need to become knowledgeable about the steps and politics involved in establishing a center in the organization and acquire skills in areas such as fundraising, grant writing, and interdisciplinary team management. As with any other objective, the mentee should write down the desired skill area as an objective, set a deadline, make a plan, and begin working on developing in that area until he or she masters it.

Both the mentor and mentee contribute to the mentoring plan's development. It begins with the mentor providing significant direction and eventually the mentee assuming more responsibility for setting and achieving goals and objectives. As original goals and annual objectives are accomplished, the mentoring relationship may end, or new goals may be established and adjusted to match how the mentoring relationship has evolved and how the junior faculty member has developed.

Finalize the Mentoring Agreement

The preparing and negotiating phases should produce a mentoring agreement, preferably in written form. The agreement includes the mentoring plan and the ground rules. Although the mentoring relationship that eventually occurs may not follow the exact agreement, it is still important for the mentor and mentee to have discussed the operational parts of their relationship and to have jointly developed a way to proceed. Whether or not the plan and ground rules are written out in detail, the process of systematically addressing these issues will greatly decrease the potential for misunderstandings and provide a solid foundation from which a positive mentoring relationship can unfold.

In summary, activities during the negotiating phase of a mentoring relationship with a new faculty member typically include the following:

- Mentee and mentor share additional background information about themselves.
- Mentee completes self-assessments.
- Mentee drafts a career vision statement and mission statement.
- Mentee and mentor discuss one another's backgrounds, review the mentee's assessment results, and discuss the mentee's vision and mission statements.
- Mentor shares information about the *institution's* vision, mission, and strategic goals.
- Mentee and mentor identify strategic goals (individual goals and goals of the department as a whole) that need to be accomplished in some specified time period to get closer to the mission and vision.
- Mentee and mentor prepare an annual plan that includes objectives, strategies, and a timeline for achieving objectives in the next year.

Instructions: Complete the following checklist to determine if you have sufficiently completed the negotiating phase.

___ 1. Accountabilities are in place for the mentor(s) and mentee.

___ 2. Expectations are clear.

___ 3. Goals are well defined and clear.

___ 4. The responsibilities of each partner are defined.

___ 5. Norms have been developed and agreed to.

___ 6. We have decided how often we should meet.

___ 7. We are in agreement about how often we should connect and who should do the connecting.

___ 8. We have articulated criteria for success.

___ 9. We have developed a workable strategy for dealing with obstacles to the relationship.

___ 10. The work plan makes sense.

___ 11. We have discussed how and when the relationship will be brought to closure.

___ 12. Our operating assumptions about confidentiality are well articulated.

___ 13. The boundaries and limits of this relationship leave enough room for flexibility.

Figure 5.4.   Checklist for the Negotiating Phase of Mentoring
From *The Mentor's Guide: Facilitating Effective Learning Relationships* (p. 115), by L. J. Zachary, 2000, San Francisco: Jossey-Bass. Copyright 2000 by Jossey-Bass Inc. Adapted with permission of John Wiley & Sons, Inc.

- Mentee and mentor identify activities that the mentor can do to facilitate the mentee's accomplishment of annual objectives and strategic goals.
- Mentor and mentee agree on mentoring ground rules.
- Mentor and mentee finalize the mentoring agreement.

Figure 5.4 is a checklist that faculty can use to ensure that they have addressed these important negotiating aspects of a successful mentoring process.

ENABLING PHASE

Now it is time to do the work to accomplish the plan. In this section we outline activities the mentor can do and topics the mentor can address to facilitate the mentee's specific plans.

Mentor Responsibilities: Provide Support, Challenge, and Vision

Regardless of the mentee's specific career plan, mentors can apply three important foundational strategies to support the work of their mentees: support, challenge, and vision (Daloz, 1999; Zachary, 2000). "Providing adequate support, appropriate challenge, and ample vision are core conditions that work together to facilitate mentee growth and development. . . . Mentors manage the relationship and support learning by creating a learning environment and building and maintaining the relationship. They maintain momentum by providing appropriate levels of challenge, monitoring the process, and evaluating progress. And they encourage movement by providing vision, fostering reflection, and encouraging personal benchmarking against desired learning outcomes" (Zachary, 2000, p. 117).

Earlier, we discussed how the mentor can assist the mentee with developing a career vision and the importance of keeping the vision in mind. A large part of helping the mentee achieve the vision involves providing support. Support is provided by building a relationship in which there is structure and the mentee is listened to and treated with respect and caring. Providing support allows the mentor to give constructive feedback to the mentee and to challenge and stretch the mentee toward the vision. Challenge is provided by such things as setting tasks, setting high expectations, and suggesting growth activities outside of the mentee's comfort zone. Bower, Diehr, Morzinski, & Simpson (1998, 1999) found that the more effective mentors used an approach that focused on career vision and that provided significant challenge paired with significant support; this approach resulted in mentee growth. Because growth that enables the mentee to achieve his or her plans is the optimal outcome of mentoring, mentors should employ high support–high challenge strategies whenever possible (Daloz, 1999).

Outcomes of Foundational Mentoring Strategies: Support, Challenge, Vision

Mentee to Mentor: "What's the best use of my time at our upcoming national meeting?"

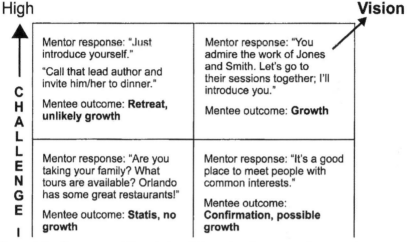

Figure 5.5.   Outcomes of Foundational Mentoring Strategies: Support, Challenge, Vision
From *Mentor: Guiding the Journey of Adult Learners* (p. 208), by L. A. Daloz, 1999, San Francisco: Jossey-Bass, and from "Support-Challenge-Vision: A Model for Faculty Mentoring," by D. J. Bower, S. Diehr, J. A. Morzinski, and D. E. Simpson, 1998, *Medical Teacher, 20*(6), p. 595. Copyright 1998 by Informa Healthcare. Adapted with permission.

Figure 5.5 is an example of how low versus high support and challenge from the mentor can result in different mentee outcomes.

Common Mentoring Strategies

No two mentoring relationships are likely to use the same strategies for developing the relationship and the mentee's career. However, research on mentoring identifies a common set of core mentoring strategies that are frequently used (Wanberg et al., 2003). Listed below is the academic version of these common strategies, with a few examples of how each might be applied.

1. *Role modeling of appropriate faculty member attitudes, values, and behaviors:*

- How to develop and maintain a professional network
- How to negotiate a difficult conversation with a colleague
- How to respond to a critical review of an article
- How to respond to student feedback on teaching

2. *Direct teaching (via readings, cases, mini-lectures, and individualized coaching) of academic competencies and norms:*
   - Academic values (e.g., academic freedom, attribution, shared governance) and the role these values have in maintaining the academic enterprise
   - Alternative perspectives
   - Unwritten "rules of the game" in the department, discipline, school, and university
   - History, traditions, governance, and leaders of the department, discipline, school, and university
   - Management of external funds, academic misconduct, and conflict of interest

3. *Providing guidance on research:*
   - Reviewing and synthesizing the literature
   - Refining a research question
   - Identifying funding sources for research
   - Preparing human subjects approval requests
   - Developing a research design
   - Preparing a data collection strategy
   - Managing data sets
   - Analyzing data and interpreting results
   - Selecting journals for results dissemination

4. *Offering the mentee a collaborative role in research:*
   - Analyzing data
   - Recruiting subjects
   - Co-authoring articles and grants
   - Identifying supplemental projects

5. *Assigning the mentee a role in teaching:*
   - Co-teaching a course
   - Precepting in a clerkship
   - Facilitating a small group

6. *Providing advice:*
   - Strategies for handling difficult work situations
   - The merits of serving on particular committees or review panels

- Where to send study data
- Finding and securing resources
- The pros and cons of different academic appointments
- Pacing work toward promotion
- Suggestions for balancing "work and life"

7. *Reviewing work and career progress:*
   - Observing and providing feedback on teaching
   - Critiquing drafts of grant proposals and research papers and presentations for national meetings
   - Reviewing drafts of curricula and teaching materials
   - Reviewing goal plans and annual performance review and promotion packets

8. *Advocating for the mentee's success:*
   - Protecting time
   - Sponsorship—nominating the junior faculty member for desirable projects, lateral moves, and promotions
   - Exposure and visibility—providing the junior faculty member with assignments that increase visibility to organizational decision makers and exposure to future opportunities
   - Protection—reducing unnecessary risks that might threaten the junior faculty member's reputation
   - Showcasing
   - Recognizing talents
   - Mediating/intervening to facilitate the junior faculty member's advancement
   - Providing opportunities for participation in professional activities
   - Providing access to key people and resources

9. *Offering encouragement:*
   - Demonstrating enthusiasm and confidence in the junior faculty member's successful future
   - Conveying positive regard
   - Serving as a sounding board
   - Reality testing
   - Nurturing the dream
   - Providing a forum in which the junior faculty member is encouraged to talk openly about anxieties and fears
   - Providing moral and emotional support

Marie Curie (seated), recipient of the Nobel Prize in Physics (1903) and the Nobel Prize in Chemistry (1911), mentor to her daughter Irène Joliot-Curie (standing), recipient of the Nobel Prize in Chemistry (1935).
Copyright the Board of Regents of the University of Oklahoma. Image courtesy of the History of Science Collections, University of Oklahoma Libraries.

- Facilitating individuality and security
- Giving special attention and positive feedback
- Interacting informally with the junior faculty member at work

Mentee Responsibilities

The mentor is not, and cannot be, solely responsible for the success of a mentoring relationship. Just as in the preparing and negotiating phases, in the enabling phase there must be a partnership in which both parties contribute to making it an effective mechanism for career success. Gordon Shea, in his book *Making the Most of Being Mentored* (1999, pp. 42–61), described the following "Seven Special Mentee Skills" that contribute to effective mentoring. He also provided a self-assessment that could alert the mentee to his or her need to increase these skills (figure 5.6).

1. *Ask productive questions.* Prepare ahead of time questions that produce the information and learning you wish to get in a mentoring exchange. Questions that are open ended versus closed (answers by yes/no or a simple one- or two-word response) are most conducive to facilitating higher-level responses and in-depth conversation.
2. *Develop key listening skills.* Listen for the central message and feelings in a response to a question. The following four steps will improve listening:
   - Listen for central ideas.
   - Determine what is of personal value to you in your mentor's conversation.
   - Identify and eliminate as many of your "trigger" words as possible. These are words that affect your mood, distract you from the conversation, and—in general —interfere with hearing the central message.
   - Use the advantage of thought speed over speech speed productively. Do not let your mind wander or mentally argue with the speaker—stay focused.
3. *Use trust-building behaviors.* Behaviors such as encouraging, listening, sharing, and cooperating are trust building, in contrast to behaviors such as putting people down, ignoring, hiding or withholding, and competing. Chapter 6 specifically addresses strategies for building trust in a mentoring relationship.
4. *Overcome the awe factor.* A mentor is likely an important person. To overcome being intimidated, prepare for the meeting, practice speaking with the person, and talk with others who have a relationship with the mentor.
5. *Resolve differences.* Use "soft" responses, such as, "That is a good suggestion, but it doesn't fit me." Use "I" versus "You" messages, such as, "I understood that we were meeting today," rather than "You missed our meeting."

EVALUATING YOUR COMMUNICATION HABITS

Advances in interpersonal communications have opened a variety of new options for mentees who wish to become more actively involved in their own development. Before going further, take a few minutes to take this communications quiz.

When meeting with your mentor (face to face, e-mail, fax, and so on) do you...

	Always	Frequently	Usually	Seldom	Never	Score
1. Communicate clearly						
2. Welcome your mentor's input (express appreciation or tell him or her how it will benefit you)						
3. Reveal your important feelings about the subjects discussed with your mentor						
4. Accept constructive feedback						
5. Practice openness and sincerity						
6. Take initiative to maintain the relationship with your mentor						
7. Actively join in to explore options with your mentor						
8. Share results with your mentor						
9. Listen for the whole message including mentor's feelings						
10. Be alert for mentor's non-verbal communications and use it as data.						

Total _____

Score yourself as follows: *Always = 10, Frequently = 8, Usually = 6, Seldom = 4, Never = 2*

If you scored below 70, you will benefit greatly by practicing the mentee skills which follow. A score of 80 or better means you are among the limited group of individuals who have good mentee interaction skills.

Figure 5.6. Evaluating Your Communication Habits
From CRISP: Making the Most of Being Mentored: How to Grow from a Mentoring Partnership. 1st ed. By SHEA, 1998, p. 46. Reprinted with permission of Course Technology, a division of Thomson Learning: www.thomsonrights.com. Fax 800-730-2215

6. *Capture the essence of your mentor's help.* After each meeting, ask yourself, "What did I learn today? How can I apply what I learned?" Summarize for your mentor what you learned, listen carefully to feedback, and ask questions to clarify.
7. *Internalize your mentor's input.* Sort out the learning and find where patterns appear. Review these in your mind shortly after they occur—substantial loss occurs in a few hours. Record the outcome of each mentoring session to reinforce your learning. Discuss the learning with others.

Ineffective Mentoring

Very rarely, a mentoring relationship is truly dysfunctional and has significant negative outcomes (Scandura, 1998). But occasionally, according to Long (1997), "under various conditions, the mentoring relationship can actually be detrimental to the mentor, mentee or both" (p. 115). Major detrimental outcomes to the mentee would result from clearly inappropriate mentor behavior such as appropriating mentee work, sexualizing the relationship, or sabotaging the mentee. Similarly, the mentor can experience negative outcomes from clearly inappropriate mentee behavior, such as gossiping with peers and disclosing confidential information about the mentor, appropriating mentor work, or discrediting the mentor in public.

Fortunately, when problems occur with mentoring, they are seldom this drastic. Ehrich, Hansford, and Tennent (2004) conducted a review of the literature on mentoring in education, medical contexts, and business. They found that problems resulting from mentoring were infrequently described in the literature. When there were problem areas, they were similar for both mentors and mentees and similar across settings (pp. 529–530). The problems most frequently mentioned by mentors were:

- Lack of time
- Negative mentee attitudes or lack of trust and cooperation
- Lack of mentor training or knowledge about the program
- Increased burden (only mentioned in medical setting)

The problems most frequently mentioned by mentees were:

- Issues of race or gender
- Cloning, conforming, or overprotection
- Perception [of the mentee] that asking for assistance was perceived as a sign of weakness or inability to cope (only mentioned in medical setting)

Mentors and mentees can avoid most of these problematic outcomes described by following the guidelines in this book. For example, problems can be avoided by establishing and maintaining a trusting, safe relationship; having commonly understood goals, clear and shared expectations of each other, stated ground rules, and frequent meetings; and attending to gender, ethnic, and generational differences. Academic leaders can assist by discussing inappropriate mentoring practices during mentoring training sessions. Mentoring programs might include an ombudsperson with whom both mentors and mentees could consult to report and resolve mentor-mentee conflicts.

CLOSING PHASE

Effective mentoring includes having a formal plan for ending the mentoring relationship and having formal closure. A closing strategy should be planned in the negotiating phase. Closure may be set to coincide with an accomplishment, such as achieving promotion or acquiring a grant. Alternatively, closure may be a specific date, such as one year after starting. Closure can also be precipitated by unexpected events, such as a lack of progress on the mentoring goals or the mentor's taking a new position. The closure may not mean the end of the mentoring relationship per se. It may be decided that the best next step is to transform the relationship by developing a new plan and continuing. Or, another option may be to add to the mentoring team and have a new mentor take a lead role, while keeping the current mentor as part of the team. Even if the mentoring experience has not been entirely positive, it is important to end the mentoring relationship on a positive note. In all cases, the first step toward closure is a review of the mentoring plan. What was accomplished? What is yet to be done? What really worked? What was not successful? What is the next phase? Evaluation is an essential component of any mentoring program.

SUMMARY

Recall that effective mentoring involves two equally important and intertwined activities: 1) career development activities and 2) relationship development activities. This chapter focused primarily on the important "business" of mentoring, that is, the phases of mentoring (preparing, negotiating, enabling, and closing) and the career development activities that occur in each phase. Careful attention to each of the phases and related activities greatly increases the likelihood of the mentee, mentor, and organization achieving the mentoring benefits described in chapter 2.

The next chapter addresses the mentoring relationship, which cuts across and undergirds all of the phases. For the phases to evolve productively and for the suggested activities to be most powerful, an effective mentoring relationship is essential. Such a relationship is one that provides the most conducive environment for faculty growth, productivity, satisfaction, and most importantly, faculty success and retention. Sometimes an effective mentoring relationship develops by happenstance, but this is not always the case. Relationships developed by chance, rather than intent, typically take longer to reach the most productive level. Thus, in the next two chapters, we discuss strategies for building an effective mentoring relationship, with particular attention to relationships that are cross-gender, cross-ethnicity, and/or cross-generation.

CHAPTER 6

Establishing Effective Mentoring Relationships, Especially Across Gender and Ethnicity

Chapter Highlights

- *Effective mentoring relationships can be challenging to develop, especially when mentors and mentees have different backgrounds and perspectives. Such differences might be more prevalent in cross-gender and cross-ethnicity matches. An awareness and appreciation of differences is needed.*
- *The literature provides insight about potential differences that might influence a mentoring relationship, especially across gender and ethnicity. For example, mentors and mentees should consider the existence and implications of unintended bias, cultural and societal norms about acceptable behavior, and the influence of family on one's career. Some women and ethnic minorities experience additional challenges in academe such as cultural taxation and feelings of isolation.*
- *To keep the relationship vital, mentors and mentees can apply strategies such as establishing trust, communicating openly and often, taking the initiative, seeing each other as individuals, and creating (then respecting) boundaries. In addition, mentors are encouraged to reflect on how power affects the mentoring relationship and to recognize mentees' potential challenges to success.*
- *In any relationship, mentors and mentees are advantaged by having an awareness of each other's unique circumstances and perspectives, be these expressed or unexpressed. As faculty become more diverse, institutions are challenged to provide mentoring*

that will encourage the retention and advancement of women and ethnic minorities in academe.

IMPORTANCE OF THE MENTOR-MENTEE RELATIONSHIP

As discussed in chapter 1, attention to developing the mentoring relationship itself is the foundation of a successful mentoring experience. The quality of interaction between mentor and mentee is critical because a quality mentoring relationship enhances mentees' attitudes toward their jobs and careers (Ragins, Cotton, & Miller, 2000). This is a highly desirable outcome for any institution seeking to attract and retain the best faculty.

Another reason to care about the quality of a mentoring relationship is that the relationship is the medium in which the mentee's learning and development takes place. It is through the personalized interaction between mentor and mentee that self-reflection occurs, career goals are set, specific competencies to be gained are identified, encouragement is given, challenges are presented, and new opportunities are explored. In short, when the mentor and mentee are interacting well, they can successfully implement the many different negotiating and enabling strategies described in the previous chapter. If the interaction breaks down—for example, is compromised by misunderstandings, damaging behaviors or attitudes, or a lack of helpful behaviors or attitudes—then the goals of mentoring are unlikely to be achieved. An environment needs to be built and maintained in which both mentor and mentee can honestly reflect, openly converse, creatively solve problems, and think critically. That environment *is* the relationship.

Relationship development activities are an important facet of any mentoring experience, but particularly so when mentors and mentees have different backgrounds and perspectives. Currently, white men constitute the majority in higher faculty ranks; therefore, they are most likely to serve as mentors. Mentees are increasingly likely to be women and minorities, especially as institutions make concerted efforts toward equity and diversity. The consequence of these circumstances is that a large proportion of faculty mentoring relationships will be cross-gender and cross-ethnicity.

Women and minorities continue to encounter additional challenges in academe that result in their being less satisfied and successful than other faculty and more likely to leave the profession (Menges & Exum, 1983; Nunez-Smith et al., 2007; Rausch, Ortiz, Douthitt, & Reed, 1989; Rosser, 2004; Rothblum, 1988; Smart, 1990). When women and minorities do stay in academe, they are much less likely to achieve the rank of full professor than are men (table 6.1). Among the challenges contributing to this "leaking pipeline" phenomenon are unintended bias, the stress of biculturalism, work-family balance, cultural and societal norms about acceptable behavior, and feelings of isolation. As faculty in higher education become more diverse, institutions must provide mentoring that successfully responds to such issues.

Developing effective mentoring relationships can be challenging, especially across gender and ethnicity. Fortunately, the literature provides helpful strategies, which we describe in this chapter. In general, these strategies are useful for all mentoring dyads or teams. But when mentoring relationships involve women and minorities, concerted mindfulness of these strategies can increase the likelihood of success.

Some of the material in this chapter is based on research designed to study specific cohorts (i.e., by ethnicity or gender). Not every mentoring relationship that includes a female or minority faculty member will require additional focus on these strategies, nor will every woman or minority face all of the challenges discussed. Each person will bring

Table 6.1. Status of Women and Minorities in U.S. Doctoral Institutions, 2004

	Gender		Race/Ethnicity	
	Women	Men	Underrepresented Minorities[a]	Other[b]
Full-time faculty	32%	68%	8%	92%
Assistant professor	41%	59%	10%	90%
Associate professor	32%	68%	8%	92%
Full professor	17%	83%	6%	94%

Note. From U.S. Department of Education, National Center for Education Statistics, 2004 National Study of Postsecondary Faculty (NSOPF:04).
[a]Includes American Indian/Alaska Native, Black/African American, and Hispanic/Latino/Latina.
[b]Includes Asian/Pacific Islander and White non-Hispanic.

a unique set of circumstances that will shape the mentoring relationship. Nonetheless, there is value in having an awareness of some of the challenges that might influence the careers of women and minorities, as well as strategies that might help them minimize or overcome these challenges.

In the United States, individuals bring *multiple layers* of historical circumstances, culture, religion, and ethnicity to their interactions with others. Thus, it is important not to make assumptions based on first impressions or basic demographic information. Knowing an individual's ethnic or cultural "phenotype" does not necessarily predict the extent to which cultural differences may be present and relevant. For example, an individual of Chinese ancestry whose family has been in the United States from the mid-nineteenth century may share little culturally with a recent immigrant from China. By contrast, members of groups historically excluded from full participation in American society (e.g., African Americans, Native Americans, women, gays, and lesbians), though residents of the United States for centuries, may still experience considerable cultural divergence from the majority population because of the history of institutionalized racism, sexism, and homophobia. Mentoring relationships—which of necessity require openness, trust, mutual expectation of fairness and benevolence, and freedom to express constructive commentary—can be complicated or hindered by cultural differences, expressed or unexpressed.

In order to acknowledge the multiple layers that make up individuals, we use the broad terms *ethnicity* and *culture* throughout this chapter. In contrast to race (a categorization more narrowly defined in terms of ancient continent of origin), ethnicity and culture encompass many characteristics, some of which include language, habits, race, and religion.

ESTABLISH TRUST

Trust is a significant factor discussed in the literature on effective mentoring, especially in regard to cross-gender and cross-cultural mentoring relationships (Bowman, Kite, Branscombe, & Williams, 1999; Brinson

**"I trust Orville immensely, just not
enough to take over the risotto."**

& Kottler, 1993; Johnson-Bailey & Cervero, 2002). When the mentor and mentee have a lot in common, they may easily perceive each other as trustworthy and predictable. In a cross-gender or cross-cultural mentoring relationship, discomfort could arise from uncertainty about the other person's culture, experiences, values, and behaviors (Thomas, 1989). The historical distrust between minority and majority group members "serves as a barrier that both must overcome to achieve the degrees of intimacy and trust that are necessary in a productive mentoring relationship" (Brinson & Kottler, 1993, p. 244).

In order to establish trust, both the mentor and mentee must strive to learn about and respect each other's perspectives and cultures (Bowman et al., 1999; Brinson & Kottler, 1993). People have different perceptions of reality, which have been formed by unique experiences. Thomas (2001) urges mentors not to subscribe to negative stereotypes of minority mentees by withholding support until the mentee proves "worthy of investment." Self-reflection is needed to be sure unintended bias does not exist. (We discuss unintended bias in more detail later in this chapter). Further, as Bowman and colleagues (1999) emphasize, minority mentees need to meet a nonminority group mentor halfway in the relationship. A deeper understanding of each other's worldviews will promote learning and growth for both parties.

COMMUNICATE OPENLY AND OFTEN

Thomas (2001) emphasizes that close relationships between mentor and mentee are important in the early career phase, "when [the protégés] needed to build confidence, credibility, and competence . . . protégés needed to feel connected to their mentors" (p. 104). Close relationships do not just happen, of course; they require conscious work, developing in large part from quality communication. For some mentoring teams, particularly those that are cross-gender or cross-cultural, communication may not come naturally. Thomas (2001) contends that cross-race relationships can be fragile, and participants may be less willing or less able to discuss sensitive issues. The same can be said of cross-gender relationships.

Open and ongoing discussion between the mentor and mentee regarding gender, ethnicity, and their corresponding barriers is one way to help bridge the gender and culture gap (Johnson-Bailey & Cervero, 2002; Thomas, 2001). Thomas (2001) encourages people to avoid "protective hesitation," the inclination to refrain from discussing sensitive issues. He performed hundreds of case studies during a three-year study of three major corporations. He found that "minorities tend to advance further when their white mentors understand and acknowledge race as a potential barrier" (p. 105) because the mentors could help mentees deal with the obstacles. He also found that minorities who advanced to executive positions had "closer, fuller developmental relationships with their mentors" (p. 104) than did minorities who did not advance to executive positions. The latter group had received only instructional mentoring, with less emphasis on the relationship itself.

It is a rare instance when two relative strangers can comfortably discuss sensitive topics early in a relationship. As a starting point for the mentor and mentee, it may be helpful to begin with conversations centered on safe topics such as the mentee's professional goals, meeting schedule, professional associations to join and functions to attend, and basic departmental, school, and university structure. After sufficient trust has been built, mentor-mentee discussions can expand to incorporate other topics, including differences in gender, culture, family circumstances, and generation.

The framework presented above is merely a guide. Conversations will take different shapes depending on the people involved. The mentor and mentee should allow a degree of flexibility in their conversations. The main message is to confront the challenges involved with the particular mentoring relationship. Open and frequent communication is the key to making the relationship supportive and productive.

TAKE THE INITIATIVE

Encourage Frequent Contact

Mentors may need to take the initiative in starting and maintaining the mentoring relationship. Brinson and Kottler (1993) view the mentoring effort as a two-way street and encourage the mentee to be proactive in the relationship as well. Yet, many mentees, including women and minority faculty, may be reticent to do so, stemming from a concern about being judged as incapable of making it on their own or being perceived as a burden to others.

A demonstration of this behavior was found in the results of focus groups conducted at the University of Pennsylvania School of Medicine (Field, 2006). Several assistant professors in this study reported they were reluctant to approach senior colleagues for mentoring. In other work, Goto (1999) wrote that because of the prevalence of the "model minority myth," Asian Americans are sometimes viewed as high achievers and not in need of mentoring, which is truly not the case. Further, she posited that Asian Americans may be concerned about burdening others and believe that the initiative for a developmental relationship will be taken by the more senior person.

Even when faculty do seek out a mentor, they may make a conscious effort to limit the amount of time they spend with the mentors.

Mentors can quell possible worries by assuring their mentees that they are invested in the relationship, are learning from it, and are committed to the mentee's success.

Facilitate Network Building

One specific way that mentors need to take the initiative is by including their mentees in networking opportunities. Networks are a vital part of a faculty member's professional development, as "standards for professional behaviour and socialisation into the profession of university academics are still largely determined by unwritten rules handed down from one generation of scholars to the next" (Wunsch, 1993, p. 354). Unwritten rules include such things as which committees are seen as important for advancement and which are not; when it is acceptable to work at home and when it is not; norms with regard to availability to students; and the number of publications expected for promotion when officially there is no specific number.

Unfortunately, research has shown that the networks of women are not as high in quality or as effective as the networks of men. This disparity results in less social capital for women, which acts as a barrier to their productivity and success (Etzkowitz, Kemelgor, & Uzzi, 2000). Using data from hundreds of interviews with faculty and doctoral candidates at research universities, Kemelgor and Etzkowitz (2001) found that, on the whole, women reported not having access to the informal professional networks available to their men peers. This led to women having more difficulty with establishing research collaborations and securing grants. In a study of tenure-track faculty at a Research I institution, the "thread running through many of the stories that women told was a sense of disconnectedness. Frequently female faculty were not invited to go out to lunch or drinks after work, or included in other important venues for informal communication" (Olsen, Maple, & Stage, 1995, p. 286).

Thomas (2001) found that strong networks were a key characteristic of successful minority executives. Social events outside of work provide a forum for fostering informal work connections among participants. Unfortunately, in Thomas's (1989) study of cross-race mentoring relationships, black and white men rarely engaged in after-work informal activities together that would typically promote career network development. Absence of collegial support not only can hinder the professional advancement of women and minorities, it could possibly isolate and frustrate them enough to leave academe altogether.

Simple acts on the part of the mentor—inviting the mentee to meetings and events, introducing the mentee to colleagues and peers inside and outside of the department and institution, encouraging the mentee to collaborate with influential others on projects, and including the mentee in informal social activities—will greatly benefit the mentee professionally. It is wise for mentors to remain mindful of taking the initiative to include mentees as appropriate networking situations arise. For mentees with young children, in particular, it is important to make these opportunities "real" by ensuring that they occur within normal work time.

Publicly Support the Mentee

Another critical *take the initiative* strategy—one closely tied to helping build the mentee's network—is public endorsement of the mentee. This is vital to increasing the mentee's confidence to take risks, network, and explore new avenues for personal and professional growth (Thomas, 2001). Women and minorities may be especially reluctant to tout their own achievements; hence, plentiful outward praise should be given and recorded when deserved. In addition, mentors can teach mentees methods of graceful self-promotion. Some common mentoring strategies related to public support (i.e., advocacy) were identified in the previous chapter.

SEE EACH OTHER AS INDIVIDUALS

There are two lenses through which the mentoring strategy of *seeing each other as individuals* must be viewed. First, through a group lens, it is important to recognize that there are differences in behavior, attitudes, and language for different groups (e.g., women and men). There is value in knowing these group differences because they can unknowingly influence our behaviors and attitudes and thereby affect our relationships. Second, through an individual lens, it is important to recognize that just because an individual identifies as a member of a group does *not* mean the individual adheres to societal expectations for that group or shares all characteristics, customs, or behaviors (i.e., norms) of that group. This point, while most easily applied to cross-gender or cross-ethnicity mentoring relationships, holds true for any mentor-mentee relationship. For example, two white women in a mentoring relationship should not assume that they approach things the same way just because they are of the same gender and ethnicity.

It is with both the group and the individual lenses in mind that we highlight next a few examples from the literature of how interpersonal styles can vary across groups. It is important that both mentors and mentees identify each other as individuals and not as representatives of a group (Bowman et al., 1999; Johnson-Bailey & Cervero, 2002), while also remaining aware of group norms and societal expectations that might be coming into play.

Interpersonal styles vary across gender and ethnicity, in part because women and minorities are allowed a narrower band of acceptable assertive behaviors (Carr, Bickel, & Inui, 2004). Heilman, Wallen, Fuchs, and Tamkins (2004) posit that "the self-assertive and tough, achievement-oriented, agentic behaviors for which men are so positively valued are typically prohibited for women" (p. 416). For example, a white man who speaks boisterously and who firmly delegates responsibilities is seen as showing qualities of authority and leadership, whereas the same behaviors from a woman cause her to be labeled "bitchy" and "unfeminine." Brinson and Kottler (1993) provide an example of a Native American professor who may be viewed as apathetic about department matters if he acts reserved in a meeting; however, his behavior may be a reflection of his cultural background. Goto (1999) points out the need to understand the silence of an Asian American mentee; she holds that mentors "should learn not to interpret the absence of questions and suggestions to mean that neither problems nor ambitions exist" (p. 59). Goto also notes that it is appropriate for mentors to encourage mentees to adopt more assertive behaviors when doing so would benefit the mentee. One should use caution, however, in determining the appropriate situations. In a study by Thomas (2001), one African American who was encouraged to mirror the aggressive style of his mentor was consequently labeled an "angry black man." Out of respect for individual differences and the narrower band of acceptable assertive behaviors allowed to women and minorities, simple clarification by the mentor such as "this approach worked for me but may not work the same for you" would be a good way of providing guidance without assuming the approach would be best suited for the mentee.

A collaborative versus competitive approach is another example of differences in interpersonal styles. The literature suggests that, in general, women operate with a more collaborative approach than do men (Rosener, 1990). Similarly, some cultures employ a more collaborative approach to tasks than the individualistic, "fend for yourself" approach held by some Americans (Cox, Lobel, & McLeod, 1991). Because people have different work styles, mentors and mentees need to have an understanding of their relative views of competition versus collaboration in work situations.

In summary, both mentors and mentees are advantaged by understanding that gender and cultural background can influence behavior and attitudes. Mentors should implement mentoring strategies that incorporate those values and behaviors. In turn, mentees may need to stretch beyond familiar behaviors to succeed. Mentors can help with this challenge but should also encourage mentees to seek additional support from successful role models and peer groups who share common characteristics (e.g., worldview, experience, gender, ethnicity, or race) (Levinson et al., 1991; Thomas, 2001). Having multiple people to provide guidance and support in a variety of personal and professional areas decreases the chance of a single mentoring relationship proving inadequate.

CREATE AND RESPECT APPROPRIATE BOUNDARIES

One of the most exciting aspects of being an academic is developing relationships with people who share similar values and passions. It is to be expected that mentors and mentees will enjoy spending time together and conversing; however, perceived risk of sexual involvement and concerns about public image could inhibit a mentoring relationship (Noe, 1988; Ragins & Cotton, 1991). In an interview by Yedidia and

Bickel (2001), one male department chair stated that male mentors "wouldn't think anything at all about working till three o'clock in the morning, you know, with a male student on something. But you might think twice about it if you're by yourself with an attractive young woman. I mean, I don't know how strong that is, but I think that a lot of faculty are very nervous about that" (p. 463). Additional dimensions might apply to cross-gender mentoring relationships that are also cross-cultural (Thomas, 1989). Similarly, discomfort can occur when mentor and mentee are of different sexual orientations.

Mentors and mentees need to set boundaries on the level of intimacy in the relationship. The goal is to maintain the relationship at an appropriate professional level without stifling the degree of trust and closeness that is needed to facilitate learning and growth. Ragins and McFarlin (1990) suggest that organizations sponsor social events where mentoring pairs can interact comfortably, without as much concern about appearance of sexual involvement. Clawson and Kram (1984) assign the responsibility of managing the closeness of the relationship to both the mentor and mentee in a quest to find "an appropriate balance of intimacy and distance that facilitates learning, growth, and productivity" (p. 31).

Once the boundaries are established, it is equally important that they are respected. It is recommended that the mentor and mentee each review their institution's sexual harassment policy. Sexual harassment is commonly defined as unwelcome sexual advances, requests for sexual favors, and other verbal or physical behavior of a sexual nature when such conduct influences employment or academic decisions, interferes with an employee's work, or creates an intimidating, hostile, or offensive work or learning environment. Should a sexual harassment claim arise, the common assumption is that a relationship cannot be consensual when there is a power differential in the professional relationship.

RECOGNIZE THE IMPLICATIONS OF THE RELATIONSHIP STRUCTURE

A power differential based on position is intrinsic in traditional and group mentoring relationships. This differential needs to be managed

"But how do you know for sure you've got power unless you abuse it?"

thoughtfully, particularly when the mentor is in a position to evaluate the mentee's professional performance (for example, when the mentor is also the department chair or a member of the promotion committee). The built-in power differential of most mentoring relationships can also affect the assertiveness of mentees who come from cultures that instill a great respect for authority and formality in its members. Cultural norms may lead a mentee to avoid asking questions, to hesitate to participate in informal interactions, and to take on any task assigned, regardless of its feasibility (Goto, 1999).

Power differentials based on social power also exist and have the potential to negatively influence mentor-mentee interactions. These differentials may be exacerbated in cross-gender and cross-cultural mentoring relationships because in many cultures the power differential between men and women and between majority and minority members is maintained through societal values. Mentors and mentees must be mindful of social power in order to minimize its impact on the mentoring relationship and on the career success of female and minority mentees.

Unfortunately, power is so historically ingrained in certain societal and structural positions that it often goes unrecognized. Kimmel states that "while individual men do not feel powerful, power is so deeply woven into their lives that it is most invisible to those who are most empowered" (as cited in Bickel et al., 2002, p. 1058). An example of the effects of socialization on our mental models is illustrated by Bakken (2005). She found that when female health-care professionals at a Midwestern Research I university were asked to envision experts in clinical research, 71 percent pictured men. Similarly, a study of male and female mentors found that women with qualifications equivalent to those of their male counterparts viewed themselves as less qualified to be mentors (Ragins & Cotton, 1993).

The effects of socialization can also be seen in how the power of mentors is perceived. A female or minority mentor may be viewed by mentees as less powerful than a white male mentor (Ragins, 1997). In a study of undergraduate students, Erkut and Mokros (1984) found that male students purposefully avoided female faculty role models and instead chose "high status, powerful male models who can promote their educational or career goals" (p. 399). Other studies similarly suggest that mentees can have difficulties accepting a mentor who belongs to a group associated by society with lower status and power (Robinson & Cannon, 2005).

Awareness by both parties of the implications of the structure of the mentoring relationship is always advantageous. Mentors, however, have an additional responsibility to seriously reflect on the power that comes with the position and how it affects their interactions with mentees. It is the mentor's responsibility to monitor how position or social power may come into play. The existence of power differentials is one reason that having more than one mentor may be beneficial to the mentee. Both mentors and mentees need to recognize and communicate openly about this issue, distinguishing appropriate position power from social power ascribed by gender and ethnicity. Together, the pair can ensure that position power and the illegitimate aspects of power based on socialization, stereotypes, and attributions do not act as a barrier.

RECOGNIZE THE MENTEE'S POTENTIAL CHALLENGES TO SUCCESS

Cultural Taxation

Cultural taxation is represented in the literature as a heavy weight on the shoulders of women and minorities in academe (Padilla, 1994; Soto-Greene, Sanchez, Churrango, & Salas-Lopez, 2005; Tierney & Bensimon, 2002). It is defined as "the obligation to show good citizenship toward the institution by serving its needs for ethnic [and gender] representation on committees, or to demonstrate knowledge and commitment to a cultural group, which may even bring accolades to the institution but which is not usually rewarded by the institution on female behalf the service was performed" (Padilla, 1994, p. 26). Often, female and minority faculty are pressured to represent their gender and ethnicity through activities such as committee work, service, and student advising. Although such roles can be fulfilling, they take time away from scholarship and other work essential to one's career advancement.

Konrad (1991) verified the reality of this situation using data from the Carnegie Foundation for the Advancement of Teaching Survey of College and University Faculty. She found that among full-time faculty, heavier academic advising and service burdens were placed upon white women and faculty of African and Hispanic origin than upon other groups in the same type of institution. Viewed frequently as tokens of their gender or ethnicity, women and minorities are handed the aforementioned tasks under the assumptions that first, they are interested in fulfilling those roles, and second, that they possess a superior knowledge of how to be effective in those roles (Padilla, 1994). Junior women and minority faculty receive a mixed message when they are subsequently not rewarded in the promotion process for their extra efforts outside of research or educational productivity (Bowman et al., 1999).

Cultural taxation should be given serious attention by mentors. According to a male department chair, "a mentor has to be somebody who says no for you . . . women and minorities . . . get asked to do every crappy little job and pseudo-leadership positions. . . . someone has to tell you which of those things are worth your time and which are not" (Yedidia & Bickel, 2001, p. 462). Mentors of women and minority mentees should be acutely aware of this implicit "responsibility" and encourage their mentees to strike a thoughtful balance so that professional accomplishment does not suffer.

Feelings of Isolation

Given the dearth of women and minorities occupying senior faculty positions, many faculty lack interaction with role models of the same gender or ethnicity (Levinson et al., 1991; Lewis-Stevenson, Hueston, Mainous, Bazell, & Ye, 2001). In an interview study of department chairs, both men and women chairs confirmed this problem for women (Yedidia & Bickel, 2001). Even in departments that include some women, being isolated from collegial networks in their departments is a common experience for women faculty, especially in the science disciplines, in which their "marginal status and collegial exclusion not only interferes with achieving complex tasks and objectives, but reduces options to deal with adversity" (Kemelgor & Etzkowitz, 2001, p. 246). The same could be said for underrepresented minority faculty.

In addition, many minorities experience internal conflict from feeling they must yield parts of their cultural identity in order to be accepted into academic society (Brinson & Kottler, 1993). Mentors can help by being open to discussion of these issues, being purposely inclusive of women and minorities in departmental collegial networks (see "Take the Initiative" section, addressed previously), and by working to change the larger system so that a greater number of women and minorities are able to advance into senior positions and become mentors and role models.

Biculturalism

Biculturalism results when "individuals learn how to maintain their dominant ethnic culture while increasing an awareness of another cultural set of values and norms" (Johnsrud & Sadao, 1998, p. 324). Minority faculty need to have both affiliations in order to succeed in the Western model of academe. The ability to be bicultural enables them to function better in the academic environment; however, "the energy required to interpret new situations places subtle pressure on ethnic and racial minority faculty who attempt to gauge appropriate responses and to shift between value structures" (Johnsrud & Sadao, 1998, p. 324).

In a study using focus groups and individual interviews with faculty at a large research university, Johnsrud and Sadao (1998) found that the stress of biculturalism presented in a variety of ways. They found, for example, that some minority faculty struggle with differences in communication styles due to cultural norms. The following response from their qualitative data set is illustrative of the communication burden and its impact on the work environment:

> The kinds of things that the faculty still in general don't do with each other [are] having the patience or the sensitivity to encourage optimal interaction with one another across cultural differences. . . . So what happens with Faculty Senate is [that] what you get is a skewed discussion from all the people who are culturally willing or at ease to speak up, and you miss all those ideas from the people for whom speaking out is not part of their enculturation. And I'm not saying there's a wide gulf but certainly subliminally it's there. (pp. 325–326)

Some minority faculty are from cultures that do not value public promotion of accomplishments, yet the tenure and promotion process requires that faculty make their efforts and successes visible. This is another example of how a faculty member may need to become bicultural in order to succeed in academe, as indicated again in the Johnsrud and Sadao (1998) study:

> Many minorities probably don't [promote themselves] because we are generally not the type that toot our own horns and that makes it very hard. Going back to promotion and tenure, yes, it is very difficult for me; it was the most difficult thing for me to sound like I'm tooting my horn, which is culturally so bizarre. It's not something that in my culture or in my own personal values I would do. I have to learn how to do it. . . . There has to be a better way of evaluating faculty for their worth and their contribution and promoting them on that basis. (p. 327)

In general, minority faculty interviewed by Johnsrud and Sadao viewed biculturalism as a necessary "survival skill," but one that came at a cost. The faculty "felt that they constantly compromised their cultural values and norms out of deference to Western values" (p. 328), yet their compromise was not reciprocated, as the majority did not work to understand their "other" perspectives. Faculty working with mentees from a minority culture should be aware of the energy that functioning biculturally demands and the frustration that can be associated with the compromise of cultural values. Both mentors and mentees can work to understand and appreciate cultural differences. In the best scenario, the mentoring dyad or team will find ways to leverage those differences to best achieve the mentee's professional goals.

Unintended Bias

Unintended biases are a function of societally defined norms and are subscribed to subconsciously by many women and men of all cultures. Despite the best efforts of mentors and mentees, unintended biases based on gender, ethnicity, age, and other factors can still exist. Unintended biases are so socially ingrained that they are often beyond conscious recognition, yet they can affect one's professional development and advancement.

The following examples illustrate the effects of unintended biases. When asked to rate their abilities on objectives related to clinical research, female postgraduate trainees consistently rated themselves lower than male postgraduate trainees rated themselves (Bakken, Sheridan, & Carnes, 2003). A study by Taylor and Ilgen (1981) showed that when asked to make job placement decisions, both women and men associated women with less challenging positions. Relative to attribution theory, Greenhaus and Parasuraman (1993) found that "among the most highly successful managers, the performance of women was less likely to be attributed to ability than performance of men. In addition, the performance of black managers was less likely to be attributed to ability and effort and was more likely to be attributed to help from others than the performance of white managers" (p. 273).

An excellent illustration of how unintended biases are manifested in academe is given by Carnes, Geller, Fine, Sheridan, and Handelsman

(2005) in their article on the selection process for the National Institutes of Health (NIH) Director's Pioneer Awards. The authors evaluated the reasons why none of the first nine award recipients were women, despite the NIH's commitment to advancing women in biomedical careers and an adequate number of qualified women applicants. They identified six elements that could have caused unintended bias to affect the selection process:

(1) time pressure placed on evaluators, (2) absence of face-to-face discussion about applicants, (3) ambiguity of performance criteria, given the novelty of the award, combined with an emphasis on subjective assessment of leadership, potential achievements rather than actual accomplishments, and risk taking, (4) emphasis on self-promotion, (5) weight given to letters of recommendation, and (6) the need for finalists to make a formal, in-person presentation in which the individual and not his or her science was the focus of evaluation. (Carnes et al., 2005, p. 684)

To support some of the elements they identified, Carnes and colleagues cite Martell's (1991) conclusions about assumptions that allow for cognitive efficiency. These assumptions, which are relied on in time pressured situations, can lead to an unintentional bias against women. In the case of the Pioneer Awards, the assumption is that men are better scientists than are women. Unintended bias can also occur by the language used. Carnes and colleagues (2005) argued that the emphasis on "risk taking," a term used implicitly in the description of an ideal Pioneer Award applicant, biases the selection process against women: "Although all innovative scientists consistently take calculated risks, being described as a risk taker would generally align with male rather than female or gender-neutral descriptive and prescriptive behaviors" (p. 688). The story changed in the second year of the Pioneer Awards. The NIH "did make a very deliberate attempt to level the playing field" by making appropriate adjustments to the competition process, according to Jeremy Berg, director of the National Institute of General Medical Sciences, who oversaw the competition (Mervis, 2005, p. 2149). Women and underrepresented minorities were encouraged to apply, only self-nominations were accepted, and the reviewers were trained "on the importance of looking for the best people with the most exciting ideas" (Mervis, 2005, p. 2149). In the second year of the program, six of the thirteen recipients were women.

Unintended biases may or may not play a role in the mentoring relationship. It is important for the mentor and mentee to recognize, however, that these biases do exist in a larger context and can have an especially negative impact on the success of women and minorities.

Success As a Barrier

"A woman's success can create new problems for her by instigating her social rejection" (Heilman et al., 2004, p. 416). Heilman and colleagues (2004) found that women who violated stereotypes by being successful at traditionally male tasks were perceived to be more interpersonally hostile than women who exhibited unclear performance and men who succeeded at the same tasks. Further, when information about level of performance at a traditionally male task was *not* provided, subjects almost always rated women as less competent and less achievement-oriented than men, as well as less interpersonally hostile. Alternatively, if women conformed to stereotype by being successful at traditionally female or neutral tasks, they were not met with disapproval by subjects. The authors concluded that the social disapproval of women who are successful at traditionally male tasks occurs because the women violate stereotype norms. It is not so much the fact that the women are successful, as it is that they are successful in nontraditional areas.

Heilman and colleagues (2004) further show that despite a woman's success, being disliked can be detrimental to a woman's career. Regardless of competence, employees who were portrayed as likable were more highly recommended for higher salaries and special opportunities than were less likable employees. It follows that if successful women in nontraditional settings (e.g., hard sciences and engineering) elicit negative social reactions, then they will be less likely to be recommended for professional advancement and other rewards. These findings substantiate the concept that even if women overcome barriers to success, it is not enough of a buffer to protect them from the effects of gender stereotypes.

Unfortunately, gender stereotyping starts early. Seymour (1995) studied undergraduate students in science, mathematics, and engineering. Female students voiced the impact that gender stereotypes had on their decisions to persist in their respective disciplines. Some of their responses reflected the difficulty of being successful and simultaneously being perceived as feminine. In terms of professional advancement, Collins succinctly makes the point that "women must guard against any impulse not to pass men" (as cited in McCormick, 1991, p. 18).

The ubiquity of gender stereotypes, erroneous attributions, and the effects of socialization present a quandary for women who strive to advance and find that, for a variety of reasons, their very success is a roadblock. Mentors who recognize this dilemma will do their best to publicly support the accomplishments of their mentees, while working diligently to dismantle the stereotypes surrounding normative behaviors based on gender.

Commitment to Family

A central issue currently affecting both women and men in academe is how to balance work and family (Acker & Armenti, 2004). Women, however, still tend to take on the majority of family responsibilities, which translates into a hefty obstacle in their professional endeavors. In a study of department chairs by Yedidia and Bickel (2001), twenty-eight of thirty-six chairs viewed the traditional gender role of caretaker for children and family as a significant barrier to the professional advancement of women. Time devoted to family matters can "often preclude [women] from devoting essential time and energies to achieving milestones that are central to favorable tenure review and promotion, and these roles limit the geographic mobility that is often necessary to advance in the profession" (Yedidia & Bickel, 2001, p. 455).

The intersection of family and professional responsibilities creates additional obstacles to success for women with children. Many women are of childbearing age during their tenure process; consequently, these "are the years when the fast track and the reproductive track are on a collision course" (Mason & Goulden, 2004a, p. 13). If women choose to have children during the tenure process, slower progress and increased stress in the quest for tenure is a likely result. From their study of full-time U.S. medical school faculty, Carr and colleagues (1998) concluded that, compared with their male counterparts, women with children had fewer publications, slower self-perceived career progress, and lower career satisfaction.

Mason and Goulden (2004b) state that "the employment structures of the professions . . . are configured for the typical male career of the nineteenth century, in which the man in the household was the single breadwinner and the woman was responsible for raising the children. According to this explanation, such rigid employment structures force women to choose between work and family" (p. 88). Their studies show that women with children, especially women who have children when in the early stage of their careers, are significantly less likely to achieve tenure, hold regular appointments, and stay in academics. Further, women who achieve tenure or hold fast-track positions make significant trade-offs in family life, such as remaining single, having fewer children than they desire, and not having children altogether. None of these effects were found for men.

Specifically, using longitudinal data from the Survey of Doctorate Recipients, Mason and Goulden (2002, 2004a) found a robust "baby gap," defined as a "consistent and large gap in achieving tenure between women who have early babies and men who have early babies [i.e., baby joins the household within five years subsequent to the parent completing the PhD], and this gap is surprisingly uniform across the disciplines and across types of institutions" (2002, p. 24). Their findings include the following:

- Women who have early babies are 24 percent less likely in the sciences and 20 percent less likely in the social sciences and humanities to achieve tenure twelve to fourteen years after earning the PhD than men who have early babies (2002).
- Women who achieve tenure are unlikely to have children in the household twelve to fourteen years after earning the PhD. The proportion of tenured women who are without children in the household at this time point is 62 percent for women faculty in the humanities and social sciences and 50 percent for women faculty in other sciences. Men in the same situation, however, are less likely to be without children in the household: only 39 percent for those in the humanities and social sciences and 30 percent in the sciences (2002).

- Women who have early babies are more likely than others to be in nonregular appointments (2002).
- Tenured women are more than twice as likely as tenured men to be single twelve years after earning the PhD (2002, 2004a).
- Only one in three women who are childless when they enter a fast-track university job will ever become a mother (2004a).

Along the same lines, using a survey of faculty members of the University of California system, Mason and Goulden (2002, 2004a) found evidence of the "tradeoff successful women make between careers and children" (2004a, p. 13):

- Women forty to sixty years old were more than twice as likely as men in the same age group (38 percent versus 18 percent) to indicate that they had fewer children than they had wanted (2004a).
- Women thirty to fifty years old and with children reported spending an average of 101 hours per week engaged in professional, household, and caregiving activities. Men with children reported spending eighty-eight hours per week in these activities, and women and men without children self-reported spending seventy-eight hours per week. For women with children, 36 percent of the time devoted to these activities is for caregiving, compared to 20 percent for men with children and less than 10 percent for men and women without children (2004a).
- Married women with children were much more likely than others to indicate that children were a reason they shifted their career away from academe. This group also was most likely to indicate that balancing career and family was a source of high stress (2002).

For women faculty, the decision to have a baby is a professional one, as well as a personal one. If they choose not to have children because of the conflicting time demands of caregiving and career, they may be sacrificing one of the most important and valuable parts of their lives. According to Acker and Armenti (2004), one woman faculty member who was considering starting a family remarked "if I have kids in the next year, how would I ever write that grant? I mean, there is a reality

... [in terms of] the number of hours you have to put in, because I'm writing three grants, trying to get my papers out, trying to keep the lab going, doing my teaching, doing the service, you know, there's no way I could have kids in the next year" (p. 11). The relationship between the tenure clock and family responsibilities is an enormous issue that affects women in academia. It is necessary for mentors to be aware of the impact of these issues on women mentees.

More and more often, the concerns of female faculty about the over-lap of family and professional responsibilities are being recognized and accepted as an institutional system issue. Suggested strategies to enhance work-life balance include improved on-site childcare in the workplace, flexible hours and leave time, delay of the tenure clock, and scheduling of meetings during more convenient times for women with childcare responsibilities (Yedidia & Bickel, 2001). Many institutions have already implemented policies related to the tenure clock for all faculty. According to Liu and Mallon (2004), by 2002, "more than three quarters (92) of U.S. medical schools with tenure systems had 'tenure-clock-stopping' policies that allow tenure-eligible faculty members to remain 'on track' but to have their probationary period extended" (p. 211). To help support mentees in this situation, mentors can advocate for these or alternative strategies to be implemented in the institution.

Beyond policy change, women should be encouraged to use the policies. They may hesitate to use them because they fear damage to their careers and being perceived as less committed (Ward & Wolf-Wendel, 2004; Wolf-Wendel & Ward, 2006). Ward and Wolf-Wendell (2004) suggest that such policies must be applied fairly, that policies be extended to men, and that both senior and junior faculty must be educated about their use. Given the considerable challenges female faculty face in terms of family demands and professional demands, mentors play an integral role by helping mentees navigate the way to professional success through a more balanced lifestyle.

SUMMARY

In this chapter, we identified a variety of relationship-enhancing practices applicable to the mentoring of higher education faculty. In describing these practices, we alerted mentors and mentees to some of the challenges that can arise over the course of a mentoring relationship, such as difficulties related to trust, communication, power, or assumptions. We specifically highlighted challenges and strategies that might be relevant to faculty in cross-gender or cross-cultural mentoring relationships.

Institutions with formal mentoring programs may wish to address some of the topics in this chapter as part of a mentor training session or mentor-mentee orientation program. It is in an institution's interest to encourage and train faculty to succeed in the mentoring role and particularly to increase the pool of mentors available to women and minority mentees. Brinson and Kottler (1993) propose that successful mentors might encourage other colleagues to engage in cross-cultural mentoring relationships. In a study of 275 executives, experience as a mentor or mentee positively predicted future intentions to mentor (Ragins & Scandura, 1999). These findings highlight the importance of initiating mentoring relationships in order to perpetuate the cycle of mentoring and spread the mentoring wealth.

The experience of mentoring or being mentored takes effort and carries with it new challenges and responsibilities, but doing so is a

Margaret Thatcher (Prime Minister of the United Kingdom, 1975–1990), mentor to John Major (Prime Minister of the United Kingdom, 1990–1997).
Reprinted with permission of the United Kingdom Conservative Party, Conservative Campaign Headquarters, Conservative Research Department.

catalyst for professional and personal growth. Thomas (2001) found that cross-race mentoring relationships allowed mentors and mentees to "explore other kinds of differences, thus broadening the perspectives of both parties" (p. 105). In qualitative research by Bland, Weber-Main, and colleagues (2005), one department head involved in mentor-mentee matching said, "I try to pair men with women and vice versa. I think there's something to be learned in both directions" (p. 76). It is important for mentors and mentees alike to remember that the primary goal of mentoring is continued growth and development, for everyone involved.

In the next chapter, we continue our discussion of effective mentoring relationships, but with a focus on another characteristic of many mentor-mentee relationships: generational differences.

CHAPTER 7

Establishing Effective Mentoring Relationships Across Generations

Chapter Highlights

- *It is not unusual, particularly in the traditional mentoring model, for the mentoring relationship to be intergenerational. Currently, many mentors are members of the Silent Generation (1926–1945) or the Baby Boomer Generation (1945–1964), whereas many mentees are Generation Xers (1965–1981) or Millennials (1982–2003).*

- *A mentor and mentee might differ in their outlook, worldview, work ethic, view of authority, leadership approach, and learning style. These and other characteristics can be significantly shaped by the era in which one grows from childhood to young adult. Examples of experiences that might be shared by a generation's members are family dynamics, societal norms, economics, and cultural trends.*

- *As is the case with gender and ethnicity, an awareness of potential differences based on age or generation (but without assuming or stereotyping) can help to establish an effective mentoring relationship. Respect for different perspectives is essential. When differences are acknowledged and valued, they can be leveraged to foster new professional skills for both the mentor and mentee.*

ATTENTION TO GENERATIONAL CHARACTERISTICS AND DIFFERENCES

Generally, the first thoughts that come to mind at the mention of diversity are gender and ethnic diversity. Age, or generational, differences are of equal importance when considering the needs of faculty and re-lationships between mentors and mentees. Generational characteristics play a large role in how people view the world, make choices, lead their lives, and interact with others. It is easy to make assumptions about people on the basis of their age and the generation to which they be-long. For faculty in intergenerational mentoring relationships, it is im-portant to understand one another's generational characteristics; these characteristics can help explain *why* people act as they do, *what* they believe and value, and *how* they approach work and life in general.

It is, of course, necessary to generalize when speaking of generations. In her work on generations, Raines (2003) states, "generalizations are helpful, as a way to begin understanding someone else, as a guideline. They give us the insights, awareness, and empathy that can lead to new cohesiveness, creativity, and productivity" (p. 11). Although individu-als have their own defining characteristics, they also have background experiences that tie them to their generation:

> From the moment of birth, we begin to be programmed—coded with data about what's right and wrong, good and bad, stylish and geeky, funny and not. As infants, we begin a series of programming experiences that create the filters through which we see the world—especially the world of work—for the rest of our lives. *A generation is a group of people who are programmed at about the same time. . . .* What gives each generation its unique character is the set of programming experiences they shared during their most formative years. (Raines, 2003, p. 10)

Not all characteristics will be different between generations. Martin and Tulgan (2002) contend that "collaboration becomes easier when different generations identify not just what separates them but also what unites them" (p. 53). Moreover, generational characteristics may be different for people of different cultures. While it is helpful to un-derstand the impact of generational membership on worldviews and behaviors, it is also necessary to remember that individuals might not relate to certain characteristics of their generation for one reason or another.

Much of the literature on generations has been written from a busi-ness and managerial perspective (e.g., Lancaster & Stillman, 2002;

Table 7.1. Generational Profiles

	Generation			
Characteristic	Silent/Veteran	Baby Boomer	Gen X	Millennial/Gen Y
Birth year range	1926–1945	1945–1964	1965–1981	1982–2003
Outlook	Practical	Optimistic	Skeptical	Hopeful
Work ethic	Dedicated	Driven	Balanced	Ambitious
View of authority	Respectful	Love/hate	Unimpressed	Relaxed/polite
Leadership by	Hierarchy	Competence	Consensus	Achievement
Relationships	Personal sacrifice	Personal gratification	Reluctant to commit	Loyal
Perspective	Civic	Team	Self	Civic

Note. Adapted with permission from Crisp: Connecting Generations 1st edition by RAINES. 2003. Reprinted with permission of Course Technology, a division of Thomson Learning: www.thomson-rights.com. Fax 800 730-2215.

Martin & Tulgan, 2001; Martin & Tulgan, 2002; Raines, 2003; Tulgan, 2000). Although some aspects of mentoring are related to managing, there is little research that focuses specifically on intergenerational mentoring for faculty. Knowledge of the background experiences and typical characteristics of each generation, however, may prove beneficial to mentors and mentees.

Table 7.1 defines the names and birth years of the generations we will discuss and summarizes some of their general characteristics. The span of birth years that mark a generation may vary by a few years in either direction depending on the source of information. Typically, generations are marked by their experiences of major societal occurrences rather than by specific years. The following sections include more detailed information about each generation and offer strategies for effectively mentoring across generations. Included in each section is a list of characteristics describing each generation, which we have compiled from references cited in this chapter.

SILENT/VETERAN GENERATION (1926–1945)

Parents of members of the Silent Generation generally raised their children with discipline and demanded obedience. Conformity and "family values" were the norms of society. In turn, members of the Silent Generation "adopted their elders' values of loyalty, dedication, and commitment to command/control leadership in hierarchical organizations" (Martin & Tulgan, 2002, p. 2). They were the ones who helped rebuild the economy in the 1950s. They worked hard for home ownership and anticipated lifetime employment with the same organization (Martin & Tulgan, 2002). In contrast to more recent generations, members of the Silent Generation did not grow up with as many choices or surrounded by as much technology.

Characteristics typical of the Silent Generation can be seen in many of its members today, as a result of the nature of their experiences during their formative years. The following list includes some of the characteristics typical of members of this generation.

- Comfortable with formality and conformity
- Value traditional forms of recognition
- Dedicated, sacrificing, hardworking, honorific, disciplined
- Respect authority and like order
- Patriotic, faithful
- Prefer face-to-face communication
- Want to understand logic behind decisions
- Believe in saving money and paying for what they get
- Patient for delayed rewards
- Embrace traditional family values
- Loyal to history of their organization and may be resistant to change

Members of the Silent Generation should be encouraged to be mentors. They possess a wealth of expertise and can be excellent resources for younger faculty. Participating in a mentoring relationship may also give the Silent Generation mentor a sense of purpose, a renewed interest in work, and exposure to the energy of a younger mentee. Martin and Tulgan (2002) note the value of cross-generational, two-way mentoring by way of their quote of a Generation X mentee to a Silent Generation mentor, "if you coach me on negotiation strategies . . . I'll teach you the latest Internet tricks" (p. 52). If the mentor and mentee can recognize and respect their generational differences, a supportive and educational mentoring relationship for both may result.

BABY BOOMERS (1945–1964)

Members of the Baby Boomer Generation are most likely to be the mentors in mentoring relationships. Born after World War II during a period of economic growth, they were raised to believe they would have a higher standard of living than their parents. They were the beneficiaries of a child-focused upbringing, hence their education was a main focus. According to Martin and Tulgan (2002), the idealism and optimism of the late 1960s and early 1970s, combined with the focus on children and families, led the Boomers to be known as the "me" generation.

Once Boomers were in the job market, the economy declined and they faced job competition and lower earnings than they had anticipated. In tandem with the downturned economy, events such as Watergate, the Vietnam War, and assassinations left the Boomers skeptical and disappointed (Martin & Tulgan, 2002; Tulgan, 2000). Boomers still held a strong work ethic, loyalty to their organizations, and willingness to pay their dues. Compared to the Silent Generation, however, Baby Boomers wanted something more real than the All-American dream. They "set out not merely to define their individuality, but to create a more open, free society" (Martin & Tulgan, 2002, p. 4). Their mixed experiences during their growth from childhood into adulthood led to the formation of the characteristics of the Baby Boomer Generation. Some of the characteristics of members of this generation are listed below.

- Loyal to jobs
- Need for security over job satisfaction
- Strong work ethic
- Used to clear job definition
- Willing to pay dues
- Want to be part of a team
- Value public recognition
- Love-hate feelings toward authority
- Narrowly focused on their own issues
- Interested in self-improvement
- Respect matters, will work hard to gain it
- Increasingly interested in work/life balance

- Growing responsibility for elder care
- Competitive
- Challenge the status quo
- Value individuality over conformity

Members of the Boomer Generation essentially connect the more experienced generations with the newest generations. They can relate to both perspectives (Martin & Tulgan, 2002). Boomers are the most recent generation of experts and potential mentors. Since many of the members of the Boomer Generation are in mid- to late-career stages, it is a perfect time for them to serve as mentors. They can help channel the energy of younger mentees, teach mentees important professional skills, and also learn from the new ideas and perspectives of the mentees.

GENERATION X (1965–1981)

Many members of Generation X are now in a position to be mentored. During childhood, they were latchkey children. More so than other generations, their parents both held jobs, had high divorce rates, and were not as focused on raising children. With unreliable family structures, a faltering economy, and a rapidly changing environment, Xers grew used to uncertainty and became highly untrusting of organizations (Bova & Kroth, 1999; Tulgan, 2000). Xers had "little reason to be idealistic—nothing in Xers' life experience has remained the same long enough to inspire [their] unquestioning belief" (Tulgan, 2000, p. 48). They learned to take care of themselves and find security in their independence. They experienced the threat of nuclear war, a society dangerous to children, an increased visibility of sex and drugs, and the AIDS epidemic. Downsizing in the early 1990s meant minimal job security for Generation Xers (Martin & Tulgan, 2002).

The following list of characteristics of Generation X members grew out of the experiences noted above.

- Highly independent, not to be mistaken for arrogance
- Used to creatively solving problems
- Want autonomy and flexibility when it comes to how to do their work

- Don't want to be micromanaged
- Not motivated by pep talks, catchy phrases, or "because I said so"
- Need their contributions to be recognized and valued
- Value recognition in the form of time off
- More likely to leave a job if not happy, will stay if job offers something valuable
- Find security in work, work can define them
- Dislike wasted time
- Value fun and informality
- Skeptical of institutions and authority, not as loyal
- Strive for work/life balance, value time with friends and family
- Desire feedback that is frequent, timely, and honest
- Entrepreneurial
- May view being mentored as a right rather than a privilege
- Don't believe in paying dues because skeptical of long-term connections
- Direct and outspoken communication style
- Need constant learning and growth opportunities
- Look out for themselves
- Comfortable with technology, realize they must keep up with the times
- Work hard when motivated, but potential of burnout
- Adaptable
- Want to be given important responsibilities
- Continuous learning and improvement is important
- Respect trustworthy mentors who lead by example

Since members of Generation X are most likely to be mentees, particular attention should be paid to the list above. Mentors from the Silent and Boomer Generations need to understand the characteristics of their younger mentees and be open minded to the younger mentees' perspectives and entrepreneurial spirits. Members of Generation X are thirsty for learning opportunities and feedback for improvement; however, they also want their independence. It seems to be a fine line, so communication between mentors and mentees regarding the workings of the mentoring relationship will be helpful.

Tulgan (2000) notes that members of Generation X may feel trusted, confident, and empowered as a result of being given increased responsibilities. This concept fits well with mentoring. Mentors can guide Generation X mentees while allowing the mentees space for autonomy and creativity in making decisions and solving problems that may arise. This approach will facilitate learning and provide the feedback that Generation X mentees desire, without making them feel micromanaged.

Bova and Kroth (2001) found that Generation X employees preferred action learning, or "the learning that occurs in the process of finding solutions to problems" (p. 60). Their second choice was incidental learning, which is a spontaneous form of learning that occurs as a by-product of a task. Their least favored approach was formal or traditional learning. Many earlier generation mentors were trained in, and learned from, the formal approach. This difference in how Generation X members prefer to learn is useful information for mentors. Generation X mentees need guidance and want to be mentored, but they prefer to learn by doing and to be as self-directed as possible.

One key characteristic of members of Generation X is that they approach distribution of their time with a focus on a healthy level of work-life balance. This approach challenges the traditional mold of an academic. Bickel and Brown (2005) contend that this desire for balance should not be mistaken for "slacking off" and that Generation Xers "may actually be extending their productive professional lives" (p. 208). Mentors in effective cross-generational mentoring relationships should help their mentees become successful in academe while incorporating their work-life balance values. Generation X mentees may also inspire their mentors to be more successful at balancing work and nonwork activities.

Bickel and Brown (2005) offer suggestions for earlier generation mentors to gain competency with mentoring Generation X mentees. Some of their techniques are quoted in the following (p. 208):

- Create a clear picture of what needs to be accomplished and divide that into achievable goals. Seek the protégé's reactions and opinions. Also, build in milestones along the way; delayed gratification resonates poorly with Generation Xers.

"Oh, like you know something the Internet doesn't know."

- Focus on outcomes. Generation Xers tend to reject the notion of obligations and prefer to have "a piece of the action," including input into the terms of any arrangement. So be clear about *what* needs to get done but leave some of the *how* to them.
- Use a participative rather than a top-down approach. A leadership style that incorporates teaching, information sharing, and engagement in problem solving is likely to be more successful than one that relies on authority or reference to "how it's done around here . . ."
- Give conscientious feedback . . . Generation Xers tend to look for and appreciate frequent, frank feedback . . .
- Encourage the protégé to mentor others. If the protégé takes the mentoring relationship for granted and underestimates the time and patience involved, encourage the protégé to become a mentor herself or himself.
- Refrain from comparing today to the glories of yesterday.

MILLENNIALS/NEXTERS/GENERATION Y (1982–2003)

Members of this newest generation are potential up-and-coming mentees. They grew up in a very child-centric environment. The structured lives of Millennials are supported by parents who are highly involved.

Members of the Millennial Generation have been given the confidence to think they can make a difference in the world and have set out to do so. Having never known a world without technology that inundates them with constant information, Millennials are constantly connected and the most technologically savvy generation. They often find themselves in positions to teach their parents, employers, and educators about technological advances. They believe education is the key to making a difference and plan to be lifelong learners. The amount of volunteer work this generation performs indicates their socially conscious collective mindset (Martin & Tulgan, 2002).

During their formative years, members of the Millennial Generation experienced terrorism, school shootings, multiculturalism, a resurgence of patriotism, and designer drugs. They are maturing in a more globalized world than ever before. Millennials are confident and optimistic. According to Martin and Tulgan (2001), "Gen Y is like Gen X on fast forward with self-esteem" (p. 18). The following is a list of some of the characteristics of members of the Millennial Generation:

- Comfortable with informal, frequent communication
- Technologically savvy, constantly connected to their network of people
- Self-confident and optimistic
- Expect a structured environment but don't want to be micromanaged
- Prefer a clear plan
- Don't believe in paying dues but expect to be highly compensated
- Believe in work as a learning experience, want to make a difference through it
- Independent and self-reliant
- Want to be respected, despite being young
- Like to be part of a team with other committed workers
- Want to collaborate at work
- Excited about learning opportunities
- Desire flexibility and work-life balance
- Want to socialize with colleagues and want work to be fun

- Socially conscious, civic-minded, likely to volunteer
- Want feedback on how they can improve, want to be mentored
- Respect authority if credible
- Entrepreneurial, hard workers
- Respond to more responsibility as reward
- Prefer an informal dress code and less emphasis on appearance
- Constantly question, won't settle until all options are explored
- Have high expectations, like to be challenged
- Achievement-oriented, want to make a difference

Members of the Millennial Generation soon will be making their way into mentee roles. Because Millennials grew up with highly involved parents, they are used to a lot of guidance and initially may feel more comfortable under the wing of experienced mentors they can respect. Mentors can help Millennial mentees not only by giving them the feedback, learning opportunities, and support they desire, but also by encouraging their independence and creativity. Mentees of this generation may also need coaching in time management skills because many grew up having their lives planned by their parents.

As a result of their research, Martin and Tulgan (2002) have compiled a list of what members of the Millennial Generation want from their managers. The following items from their list are equally applicable to mentoring relationships (pp. 38–39):

- Spend time getting to know them and their capabilities
- Focus on work but be personable and have a sense of humor
- Treat them as colleagues who are at work to add value
- Be respectful and call forth respect in return
- Consistently provide constructive feedback
- Let them know when they've done a good job

Members of this newest generation will bring a voracious appetite for learning and an incredible energy to their work. Mentors should not be surprised when Millennial mentees question everything. "This constant questioning is the product of lifelong exposure to the diverse viewpoints and infinite possibilities presented by technology and the information tidal wave. Gen Yers have been bombarded by endless choices and options. They've been challenged by diverse core beliefs, opinions, and points of view. They're often unwilling to settle for one solution until others have been explored. And this is, of course, the prerequisite for innovation" (Martin & Tulgan, 2001, p. 24). This is good news for the future of higher education.

SUMMARY

Intergenerational mentoring can be an invaluable experience for mentors and mentees alike. Both generational similarities and differences can be positive contributors to a successful mentoring relationship. In the spirit of Martin and Tulgan (2002), members of different generations should "respect and honor [their] differences and approach them not as a reason for conflict but as springboards to learning, productivity, and innovation" (p. 56).

This leads us to our next chapter that addresses mentoring for mid-career and senior faculty. The development of this "older" generation of faculty is often neglected but is an integral part of any mentoring initiative.

CHAPTER 8

Mentoring Midcareer and Senior Faculty Members

Chapter Highlights

- *The case for mentoring midcareer and senior faculty is multifaceted and compelling. These highly productive faculty are desirable recruitment targets, and mentoring can help retain them. At the same time, it is these faculty who are called upon to provide a supportive climate and mentoring for new faculty. Mid- and late-career is also a time when many faculty want to give back to their organization. Mentoring can be used to help faculty prepare for, and succeed in, their new roles and responsibilities.*

- *Midcareer and senior faculty are frequently in transition with regard to their goals and how they spend their time. Because mentoring can readily be individually tailored, it is an optimal strategy for helping faculty to make successful transitions.*

- *Midcareer and senior faculty do have some common needs, which mentoring can help address. Examples of these needs are a desire for new opportunities for intellectual inquiry and for the flexibility to focus on one's area of greatest professional interest.*

- *Peer and group mentoring are suitable models for midcareer and senior faculty. A formal approach is desirable. By creating mentoring programs for faculty at different career stages, institutions can help all faculty to remain motivated, satisfied, and productive and to set goals that are well aligned with those of the institution.*

REASONS TO MENTOR MIDCAREER AND SENIOR FACULTY

Much of the focus of this book has been on mentoring for new faculty members. The reason for this is twofold. First, early faculty success increases the likelihood of career-long success and retention. Second, many more new faculty will need to be hired in the coming decade as a larger number of current faculty, hired during the higher education expansion of the 1960s and early 1970s, begin to retire.

These reasons for supporting the success of new faculty members do not relieve institutions from finding ways to support their more experienced faculty. To the contrary, it is critical that institutions do just that. Consider the following:

- "Midcareer" is a long career stage. As many as twenty to thirty years can elapse between achieving the first promotion and even beginning to think about retirement, and more and more faculty are experiencing these years at the same institution.
- Without attention to their career vitality, midcareer and senior faculty could experience an unwelcome plateau in their work life. This might occur, for example, if they do not keep up with the continual knowledge and technology explosion, or if they experience a sense of declining options for scholarly contributions as they proceed through career stages (American Association for Higher Education Task Force, 1984; Finkelstein, 1996).
- Mid- to late-career is a time when faculty members have experience on which to build and a desire to contribute to and influence the organization. Many of the features of a vital organization (e.g., leadership and maintenance of a cohesive culture and positive climate; see chapter 4) depend on midcareer and senior faculty. These faculty are also key players in the recruitment and successful transition of incoming faculty (Berberet, Brown, Bland, Risbey, & Trotman, 2005).
- For most institutions, economic trends have meant only minimal monetary rewards for outstanding performance by midcareer and senior faculty and limited funding for professional development activities. These conditions can negatively affect the vitality of

these faculty (Bland & Bergquist, 1997; Caffarella, Armour, Fuhrmann, & Wergin, 1989; Karpiak, 1996).

• Attending to the vitality of faculty across the career span can help prevent the tremendous financial costs that are incurred when a productive midcareer or senior faculty member leaves to take a position in another academic institution or in the nonacademic sector (Demmy, Kivlahan, & Stone, 2002; Steele, 2006; Wingard et al., 2004). We presented examples of these costs in chapter 3. For reasons such as these, it is essential that institutions proactively attend to the continued growth and development of all faculty, even as they grow in experience and succeed in accomplishing their initial career goals. Notably, the developmental needs of midcareer and senior faculty can be challenging to address. A key difficulty is that their needs are not as obvious as those of entering faculty and are more variable across individuals.

Mentoring, which is readily tailored to the individual, is a powerful tool for facilitating faculty vitality over the entire career span. To illustrate the enduring value of mentoring for higher education faculty, we first provide information about how a faculty member's work life changes as he or she enters the later stages of an academic career. We follow this with a brief overview of some of the professional needs held in common by senior faculty. Finally, we describe how the different mentoring models and processes described in earlier chapters apply to the career development of more experienced faculty.

DYNAMIC NATURE OF MIDCAREER AND SENIOR FACULTY LIFE

What is known about the midcareer and senior faculty stage? For many faculty members, midcareer is an exciting period, with tremendous opportunity. The press of being on probation is over, the ropes of academe are now familiar, and there is confidence as a result of having achieved initial goals. From the perspective of the individual faculty member, midcareer is a time of relative freedom to pursue dreams, with much of one's career still ahead.

In *The Vitality of Senior Faculty Members: Snow on the Roof—Fire in the Furnace* (1997), Bland and Bergquist looked to adult development theory to set a broader context for understanding midcareer and senior faculty life. Levinson's (1986) theory of adult development suggests that these years are ones of constant transition, with ongoing questioning and reassessing of priorities. This is consistent with Super's (1986) work on career development; he found that while midcareer is a time of relative stability, it is also a time when "career recycling" occurs as one adjusts to new circumstances and opportunities. All of this suggests that midcareer is a very dynamic time in which faculty will be continually developing and reinventing themselves. Indeed, Seldin (2006) found in his survey study that midcareer faculty are thinking about whether to stay the course or change career paths.

Another study by Baldwin, Lunceford, and Vanderlinden (2005) confirmed the dynamic nature of midcareer and senior faculty life. This research used one of the largest national samples of higher education faculty, the National Study of Postsecondary Faculty (U.S. Department of Education, 2002). The investigators clustered faculty, who ranged in age from thirty-nine to sixty years old, into four life stages. They found that the work life and activities of midcareer and senior faculty are very different from those of junior faculty and the activities change as the faculty member moves across life stages. For example, article productivity is higher in early and middle years, whereas book productivity is higher in late career. Time spent on administration is higher in middle years, but time spent on teaching is higher in later years.

In short, midcareer and senior faculty are frequently in transition with regard to how they spend their time, the products they produce, and on the goals on which they are focused. Providing strategies to support these transitions is challenging.

NEEDS OF MIDCAREER AND SENIOR FACULTY

Several writings have identified the common needs of midcareer and senior faculty. For example, a survey of the needs and perspectives of "late-career" faculty (age fifty years or older) was conducted at the

"All of a sudden, everyone seems younger than I am."

University of North Carolina (sixteen campuses), the Association of New American Colleges (twenty campuses), and the University of Minnesota (four campuses). This study found that senior faculty needs are intertwined within three issues: motivation and satisfaction, stress, and retirement plans (Berberet et al., 2005).

Motivation and Satisfaction

A variety of factors, many of them intrinsic incentives, influence the motivation and satisfaction of senior faculty (Berberet et al., 2005). For survey respondents, two of the most highly rated items were intellectual stimulation in one's discipline and the opportunity to make a positive impact on one's institution. The authors further noted, "Overall, these survey results are consistent with other studies of faculty motivation and satisfaction [Wergin, 2001] which rank intellectual inquiry at the top, followed by desire for membership in a meaningful academic community, to have institutional impact, and to be recognized for one's work" (Berberet et al., 2005, p. 87.)

Stress

Senior faculty in this study also underscored many ways in which academic work contributes to faculty stress (Berberet et al., 2005). Notably, their sources of stress are very similar to those reported by new faculty, which we describe in chapter 4. They include a lack of time to give a piece of work the attention it deserves and inadequate institutional acknowledgment and rewards for service. Other key sources of academic stress for this late-career faculty sample were the difficulties associated with balancing the time demands of teaching and research and the challenges inherent in institutional processes and procedures (e.g., "red tape").

Retirement Plans

Senior faculty members in the study indicated that they would likely retire earlier than expected if they were dissatisfied with their work environment, not performing their job up to their expectations, feeling unappreciated by their departmental or institutional colleagues, or facing increased workload and productivity expectations at their institution (Berberet et al., 2005). Conversely, senior faculty respondents reported that they would be influenced to retire later if they experienced high satisfaction from their work and had access to flexible workload policies that would allow them to focus their efforts on areas of greatest professional interest.

MENTORING STRATEGIES FOR MIDCAREER AND SENIOR FACULTY

Mentoring is an effective approach for supporting career transitions and addressing psychosocial areas such as stress, motivation, and satisfaction. It is also a strategy that can be easily tailored to individual needs. Thus, mentoring can be a particularly effective strategy for maintaining the vitality of midcareer and senior faculty. Wheeler and Wheeler (1994) reported on a mentoring program at the University of Nebraska that was "specifically designed to help midcareer faculty reassess and refocus their careers" (p. 96). Mentoring continues to have value as a

Formal Approaches to Midcareer and Senior Faculty Mentoring

Informal peer mentoring of sorts has long occurred among midcareer and senior faculty. But Belker (1985), an early researcher on mid- and late-career vitality efforts, argued for a formal approach. On the basis of a review of the literature and existing programs for midcareer faculty at that time, he concluded that it is important to integrate individual development with institutional goals so that development efforts do not become "tangential, even superfluous to the larger tasks facing universities and colleges. . . . Faced with an older faculty, limited opportunities to hire new faculty, and fiscal restraints, colleges must begin to confront the issue of [ongoing development] . . . as a concept that will mutually benefit the faculty member and the institution" (pp. 69, 71).

A proactive effort by the institution facilitates peer mentoring. This point was revealed to the authors of this book in a series of focus groups with several senior faculty to discern what support they would find helpful at this stage of their career. These groups included former department heads, nationally recognized researchers, and endowed professors—all longtime leaders. A surprisingly large number of them were feeling out of sync with the organization, no longer valued, isolated, and lonely. The focus groups quickly moved from the planned agenda to a peer mentoring session in which participants talked together for the first time about their careers, providing suggestions and coaching for each other. Some of the issues brought up during these conversations were as follows:

- I don't quite know how to contribute to my department since I stepped down as chair. I don't want to get in the way of the new chair. What have others done?
- I really want to shift my research from basic to translational research. Is that possible?
- I want to have a meaningful, broad institutional role before I retire. I think I have learned a lot about how this place works, but I am afraid to say out loud that I am interested in administration.
- If you think talking administration is scary, try retirement. If I bring that up in my department, people will start measuring my office space for their furniture.

These people saw each other every day in the halls and at meetings. But it took legitimizing a conversation about their careers for even this small bit of peer mentoring to happen.

Even the most successful, experienced faculty member can run into obstacles over the course of a long academic career. In their interview study of leaders of highly research-productive departments, Bland, Weber-Main, and colleagues (2005) identified several common obstacles that could, if not attended to, significantly diminish a faculty member's vitality in the mid-to-later stages of one's career. Among these obstacles were "lost spark" (a faculty member becomes burnt out or disillusioned); lack of sufficient time to devote to academic work; a substantial change in work environment that causes stress and uncertainty; and diminishing resources, such as when one's longtime research area is no longer a priority of external funding agencies (p. 171). Here, too, is where formal mentoring can be of help. Mentors of midcareer and senior faculty can play a major role in brokering opportunities for their mentees so that potential obstacles are prevented or quickly overcome, and career goals are met. For instance, mentors can encourage mid- to senior-level mentees to take sabbaticals, recommend appropriate workshops for training in new skills, help make connections to colleagues in another discipline, or nominate mentees for prestigious awards.

Overall, midcareer and senior faculty are likely to encounter a wide variety of challenges and opportunities throughout their careers, including challenges related to changes in their work roles, time commitments, research focus area, teaching emphasis, and more. Consequently, they—and certainly their institutions—would greatly benefit from some type of formal mentoring to help them negotiate these transitions successfully. For example, an institution might support mentoring groups for midcareer and senior faculty on topics such as the following: How does one make a shift in research focus midcareer? What are the opportunities for leadership or to have institution-wide impact in an area? What should one consider when thinking about retirement? How does one change work activity, for example, from research to educational leadership or administration? (Mentoring for faculty who are considering an academic leadership role is the topic of chapter 9.)

Applying the Mentoring Process to Midcareer and Senior Faculty

In peer and group mentoring for midcareer and senior faculty, the purpose of mentoring conversations is the same as for any mentoring relationship: to facilitate self-development. The only difference in this situation is that all faculty are likely to serve in both the roles of mentor and mentee.

In chapter 5, we described in detail the phases of a mentoring relationship using language and examples most useful for traditional mentoring, in which the mentee is a junior faculty member and the mentor(s) is an accomplished senior faculty member. These phases are preparing, negotiating, enabling, and closing. With midcareer and senior peer or group mentoring, it is still important to pay attention to the essential tasks of each phase, but the tasks will need to be handled differently. For example, in the negotiating phase, participants learn about each other's background. In the case of midcareer and senior faculty, they may have known each other and worked together for twenty years. Still, it is important not to assume that these faculty know what they need to about each other for mentoring. Also, even with midcareer and senior faculty, it is important to attend to the ground rules and confidentiality issues of mentoring, so that everyone has the same understandings and expectations.

Recall, when developing the mentoring plan in a traditional mentoring model involving a senior mentor and junior mentee, we suggested addressing four parts:

- *A career vision statement* that describes what the world looks and feels like as a result of the mentee doing his or her work.
- *A career mission statement* that defines what the mentee will do in order to achieve his or her vision.
- *Strategic goals statements* that describe what the mentee wants to accomplish in his or her career in the years ahead in order to achieve the mission and vision.
- *Annual plans with timelines and outcomes* that delineate the mentee's concrete plans for next year's work.

These same four elements of a mentoring plan can be used with midcareer or senior faculty, particularly if the mentee is working on a career transition. If these do not seem the best fit for the concerns of a midcareer or senior faculty member, it may be easier to use the following questions to guide the mentoring process (Rolfe, 2006):

1. Where am I now?
2. Where do I want to be?
3. How do I get there?
4. How am I doing?

Figure 8.1 shows how these four questions guide a mentoring process. When a peer group member is in the role of mentor, the first task is to help the mentee assess his or her current situation, personal strengths and weaknesses, and interests. Next the mentor facilitates the exploration of future options and the eventual setting of goals. Then, the peer mentor and mentee develop strategies for achieving the goals, such as possible resources, training, time, and support needed. Finally, the peer mentor encourages and supports the mentee as the plan is implemented and helps to monitor the progress toward the established goals.

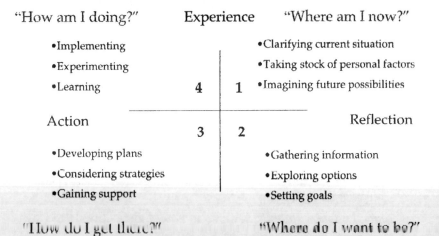

"How am I doing?"   Experience   "Where am I now?"

•Implementing			•Clarifying current situation
•Experimenting			•Taking stock of personal factors
•Learning	**4**	**1**	•Imagining future possibilities

Action			Reflection
	3	**2**	
•Developing plans			•Gathering information
•Considering strategies			•Exploring options
•Gaining support			•Setting goals

"How do I get there?"   "Where do I want to be?"

Informed Decisions

Figure 8.1.   The Mentoring Conversation
From *How to Design and Run Your Own Mentoring Program* (p. 20), by A. Rolfe, 2006, Terrigal, Australia: Mentoring Works, A division of Synergetic People Development Pty Limited. Reprinted with permission of author.

SUMMARY

Midcareer and senior faculty are constantly changing and developing. Academic leaders can leverage the versatility of mentoring to help faculty maintain their vitality from first appointment to retirement. When using peer or group mentoring with midcareer and senior faculty, all of the phases need to be attended to, just as in traditional mentoring. The strategies used in each phase, however, must be tailored to the diverse mentoring needs and greater experience of this faculty subset.

Most faculty at one time or another will encounter obstacles that might stall their academic work or dampen their passion. Mentoring can help midcareer and senior faculty to overcome such obstacles by keeping them connected to their peers and their organization, sustaining their motivation, and enhancing their productivity and satisfaction. Whether mentoring occurs in groups, pairs, or some combination, it is important that institutions support the mentoring effort. Both the institution and the individual faculty member benefit when the organization provides a structure and opportunities for faculty to mentor one another through the complexities of each career stage.

For some midcareer and senior faculty, the next career stage involves a transition into academic leadership. A career shift of this type will engage faculty in different roles, require new competencies, and induce substantial changes in their work life. In the next chapter, we discuss the ways in which mentoring for leadership can help faculty successfully navigate this transition.

CHAPTER 9

Mentoring for Faculty Considering Academic Leadership Positions

Chapter Highlights

- *A subset of successful faculty will direct their careers toward service in the form of academic leadership and administration. For these mentees, the ideal mentor is a successful academic administrator who has made a similar transition—a leader who understands the rewards and challenges of the position, its expected roles and responsibilities, the different constituencies to whom a leader reports, and the competencies needed to succeed.*
- *Administrative leadership positions will engage faculty in new or expanded roles and competencies (e.g., conflict resolution, financial management, fundraising, strategic planning). The shift from traditional faculty roles can also prompt significant changes in a faculty member's daily work routines and relationships with colleagues. For faculty thinking about a career change of this magnitude, careful consideration of these issues is an important step in the mentoring process. Mentors can also help faculty to discern their motivation for seeking a new role.*
- *Effective mentoring for leadership will likely require multiple mentors (often drawn from outside the institution). Moreover, these mentoring relationships may need to be varied in their configuration. Mentees will benefit from a tailored mix of short- and long-term mentoring support, with attention to their career goals as well as mentoring for specific competencies to help them succeed in their new work roles.*

- *Overall, mentoring can have a tremendous impact on a faculty member's career development, and particularly so during times of actual or potential career transitions. This is especially true for faculty considering a leadership position.*

INTRODUCTION

This chapter focuses specifically on mentoring for faculty who are considering, or who have just begun, a leadership position in academic administration—for example, division director, department chair, or dean. Academic leadership can be a very creative and satisfying career direction for mid- to senior-level faculty seeking the opportunity to shape higher education beyond the scholarship of their discipline. The shift to administration, however, does represent a major career change from the traditional faculty role. Important differences are the additional range of competencies necessary for leadership roles, the broader and more diverse constituencies to whom academic leaders must report, and aspects of professional life such as control over work time and the nature of one's relationships with colleagues.

Faculty who wish to prepare themselves for an administrative position in higher education can benefit greatly from having an experienced, informed "thinking partner" (i.e., a mentor) to help them process the data required to make a career transition. Many of the general mentoring principles that we discussed in previous chapters will still apply to this particular mentoring situation. But there are also many distinct ways in which a mentor can help a faculty member to thoughtfully consider this potential role transition and then identify strategies for successfully negotiating the role change.

We begin this chapter by describing some of the unique aspects of the mentor's role when the mentee's goal is to assume a new leadership position (in contrast to mentoring for success in the traditional faculty role). Then, we summarize how the general mentoring principles from previous chapters still apply, either directly or with modification, when mentoring for a transition to leadership. As examples, we use the transition to the role of department chair or dean, although the basic mentoring process will be similar for other positions as well. We provide an illustrative overview of the roles and competencies necessary to be a successful department chair or dean, compare how the professional lives of these administrators differ from those of faculty, and discuss the role of mentoring in facilitating this type of career transition.

UNIQUE ASPECTS OF MENTORING FOR A TRANSITION TO LEADERSHIP

In developing this book on faculty mentoring, we began with the implicit assumption that the mentee has already decided upon a career in academe and is actively engaged in the profession as a faculty member. Given this assumption, we focused our content on specific ways that institutions and individuals might successfully use mentoring as a strategy to help faculty remain highly productive and satisfied in all of their traditional roles, throughout their careers.

A subset of these successful faculty will have the professional goal of assuming a position in higher education administration. In this case, the ideal mentor is a successful academic administrator who has made a similar transition. There are many ways in which an experienced academic leader can help a faculty member thoughtfully approach the potential transition. Specifically, mentors can help mentees to do the following:

- Discern why she or he is interested in the leadership position.
- Understand the roles, tasks, and responsibilities of a particular position.
- Identify the competencies needed to fulfill these leadership roles and select strategies for acquiring (or strengthening) the necessary competencies.
- Understand the nature of the professional lives and daily routines of those serving in a particular leadership position.

Each of these mentoring roles is briefly described next.

Discern Reasons for Interest in a Leadership Position

The first role of a "leadership mentor"—a mentor sought to help a faculty member transition to a new leadership role—is to help the mentee identify precisely why he or she wants to make the transition. Perhaps something is missing from the faculty role, the mentee needs a new challenge, the mentee sees the transition as a way to accomplish a broader vision, or others are "calling" on him or her to take on this role. When considering a major transition, it is imperative that the decision is made based on sound rationale and not as a reaction to frustration or lack of direction.

Irene W. D. Hecht, who has directed the American Council on Education Department Chair Leadership Programs since 1992, stated that there are three main reasons a faculty member may consider assuming a department chair position:

1. The desire to be the good citizen by taking a turn at doing an unenviable task.
2. The conviction that one can do something beneficial for the department.
3. The lure of personal growth as one meets new challenges (Hecht, 2006, p. 2).

Hecht also found that the rewards of being a department chair fall into three categories:

1. Enjoyment of seeing "good things happening" in the department.
2. Excitement about contact with a bigger world.
3. Sense of pleasure from mastering new challenges (Hecht, 2006, p. 9).

Taking on the role of a chair to be a good citizen most often occurs in the case of small departments in which the chair position is rotated among the faculty. Even in these cases, faculty may welcome this opportunity as a way to make a larger contribution to the department. A person drawn for this reason often has specific goals or initiatives in mind that are best achieved from a position of higher leadership.

For a faculty member who is seeking to accomplish a larger mission and is looking for new challenges, the role of a leader can be very attractive.

Understand the Roles, Tasks, and Responsibilities of the Leadership Position

If the mentee's reasons and reward expectations are a match with a leadership position, the mentor should encourage the mentee to gather information about the position. Specifically, the mentee needs to know the roles and responsibilities of the position.

The primary roles of a faculty member are teacher and scholar, although faculty often participate in other related roles, such as provider of institutional service, educational course coordinator, discipline-related community outreach, or professional service (e.g., patient care for health professional faculty, legal services for law school faculty). The previous chapters focus on how to help faculty acquire the skills, networks, and socialization needed for success in these traditional academic roles.

The roles of an academic leader are significantly different from those of a faculty member. Further, they vary considerably depending on the particular position (chair, dean, provost, vice president, or president) and setting (institution type and size). For example, medical school department heads in large, research-oriented institutions often have responsibility for large budgets and large numbers of faculty who teach, conduct research, and practice medicine. These department heads are responsible not only for the education and research that occurs in the department, but also for the success of a multimillion-dollar clinical business enterprise with significant risk management issues. In contrast, a chair of a humanities department in a small liberal arts college is typically responsible for a smaller number of faculty and fewer resources. The diverse nature and responsibilities of academic leadership roles are further complicated by the fact that these leadership roles have changed over time and will continue to evolve as higher education institutions adapt to changes in the environment in which they function (Montez, Wolverton, & Gmelch, 2002).

The differences in leadership roles extend to the selection process for different positions. For example, the chair or head of a medical school department is identified via a national search, appointed by the dean, and expected to serve as long as performance merits. This is in contrast to the typical pattern in a college of liberal arts where a department chair is usually elected by the faculty (with the dean providing final approval) for a specified term, with the expectation that after that time has expired, he or she will return to the faculty.

Given that aspects of a leadership position will differ depending on the context, faculty members with an interest in leadership should identify the position of interest to them and expand their mentors to include someone experienced in this type of position. A clear understanding of the roles, tasks, and responsibilities is essential. This information can be gathered from multiple sources, including current and past administrators in a similar context within and outside of the institution, members of the department or college, and higher-level administrators.

Many authors have compiled lists of typical department chair and dean roles, tasks, responsibilities, and competencies. For example, "Tucker (1984) suggested that chairs have the power and responsibility to influence institutional policies and procedures; recommend faculty for appointment, promotion, and tenure; control budgets, class schedules and teaching assignments; affect student interaction with the institution; and establish and maintain departmental culture" (Wolverton, Ackerman, & Holt, 2005, p. 228). Others have developed slightly different lists, such as Carroll and Gmelch (1994) who identified fifty-four tasks, and Creswell, Wheeler, Seagren, Egly, and Beyer (1990) who identified ninety-seven tasks. Similarly, many authors have tried to describe the tasks and responsibilities of deans (Jackson, 2006; Wolverton, Gmelch, Montez, & Neis, 2001).

Table 9.1 displays a list of typical faculty, chair, and dean responsibilities. The major responsibilities for faculty were identified via a search of the literature and a national survey of successful faculty members in academic medicine (Bland, Schmitz, Stritter, Aluise, & Henry, 1990; Stritter, Bland, & Youngblood, 1991). The chair task list is based on a literature review and was further refined via a study of eight hundred department chairs (66 percent response rate) at one hundred research and

Table 9.1.   Profile of Typical Responsibilities of Faculty, Department Chairs, and Deans

Responsibilities in:	Faculty[a]	Department Chair[b]	Dean[c]
Direct Educational Work (Teaching)	XXXX[d]	XX	—
Research	XXXX	XX	X
Personal Scholarship	XXXX	XXX	X
Educational Administration	X	XXXX	XXX
Oversight of Institutional Educational Programs	—	XXX	XXXX
Research Administration	X	XX	XXX
Oversight of Institutional Research	—	X	XXXX
External and Political Relations	—	X	XXXX
Resource Development	X	XX	XXXX
Resource/Budget Management	X	XXX	XXXX
Resource Allocation	—	XXX	XXXX
Fund-raising	X	XX	XXXX
Institutional Vision/Mission	—	XX	XXXX
Institutional Growth	—	—	XXXX
Leadership	X	XXX	XXXX
Faculty Development	—	XX	XXXX
Personnel Management	X	XXX	XX

[a]From "Determining Essential Faculty Competencies," by F. T. Stritter, C. J. Bland, and P. L. Young-blood, 1991, *Teaching and Learning in Medicine*, 3(4), pp. 232–238.
[b]From "A Comparison of Department Chair Tasks in Australia and the United States," by M. Wolverton, W. H. Gmelch, M. L. Wolverton, and J. C. Sarros, 1999, *Higher Education*, 38(3), pp. 333–350.
[c]From "The Roles and Challenges of Deans," by J. M. Montez, M. Wolverton, and W. H. Gmelch, 2002. *The Review of Higher Education*, 26(2), pp. 241–266.
[d]Level of responsibility in areas range from: none—; to some x; to extensive XXXX. This table describes some, but not all, differences in responsibilities of faculty, chairs, and deans.

doctorate-granting I and II institutions (Wolverton, Gmelch, Wolverton, & Sarros, 1999). The dean task list was compiled from a survey of 1,370 deans (60 percent response rate) in colleges of education, business, liberal arts, and nursing in sixty public and sixty private institutions (Montez et al., 2002). A review of lists such as these illustrates the very different roles of leaders compared to faculty members. An understanding of these differences can help faculty identify areas for which new mentorship or specific skills training is required.

Identify and Acquire Competencies Needed to Fulfill the Leadership Roles

For faculty interested in taking on a new leadership position, the next steps are to identify the following: 1) the competencies needed to fulfill the role, 2) which of these competencies the mentee already possesses, 3) which competencies need to be acquired, 4) strategies for acquiring necessary competencies, and 5) what intermediary positions are helpful, expected, or required.

As mentioned previously, the specific leadership competencies needed will vary depending upon the nature of the institution, discipline, and specific position. Appendix D provides an example of essential competencies for medical school deans. These competencies were identified via a review of the literature and used as the basis for the development of a national program for preparing faculty for dean-level or other higher-level positions in academic medicine. There is a rich abundance of journal articles and books on leadership in higher education with other examples of the roles, responsibilities, and essential competencies for department chairs, deans, and other academic leaders. In addition, there are periodicals with this focus; for example:

- *The department chair: A resource for academic administrators* (newsletter) Anker Publishing, Williston, VT, 01740-0249.
- *Effective practices for academic leaders* (newsletter), Stylus Publishing, Sterling, VA, 20166.
- *Academic leader: The newsletter for academic deans and department chairs*, Magna Publications, Madison, WI, 53704.
- Henry, R. (Ed.) *Transitions between faculty and administrative careers*. New Directions for Higher Education, Vol. 134. Hoboken, NJ: John Wiley & Sons, 2006.

It will be useful for the mentor and mentee to review the competencies required for success in the given administrative role. The mentor should then facilitate ways to help the mentee acquire missing competencies. The mentor can advise the mentee to participate in activities that will help develop an academic leadership portfolio (e.g., chairing a major committee or leading a special task force), thereby positioning the mentee for future administrative leadership positions. Taking on a series of smaller but incremental administrative roles is a strategy by which a faculty member can get on-the-job training to expand his or her abilities and administrative experiences. This strategy both provides preparation for a successful transition and provides an evaluative exercise for the faculty member to help assess whether movement into administration is a good fit (see Strathe & Wilson, 2006; Wolverton et al., 2005).

Additionally, there are many training and development programs for faculty considering or just entering an administrative position. On a national scope, the American Council on Education offers leadership and professional development programs for each level of leadership from chair to president (see http://www.acenet.edu/Content/NavigationMenu/ProgramsServices/CEL/index.htm). Several other national programs exist such as Harvard University's Institute on Management and Leadership in Educational Institutions and the Higher Education Resource Services (HERS) program at Bryn Mawr College. National associations, such as the National Association of State Universities and Land Grant Colleges, also offer programs, as do specialty discipline

"I've got some skills—I'm just not sure they add up to a 'set.'"

associations. For example, the Association of American of Medical Colleges has a mentorship program for aspiring deans as well as leadership development programs for associate deans and department chairs. On a more local level, many larger institutions have on-site opportunities for employees to develop administrative skills.

Understand the Professional Lives of Academic Leaders

Faculty who are considering a transition to a leadership position must recognize that life as an administrator is quite different from life as a faculty member. Professional roles, work routines, and relationships are a few of the areas that will be affected by such a transition. Mentors can help mentees to recognize these differences and consider the impact of drastic changes in their professional and personal lives. Further, mentees should be encouraged to think about what it will mean to leave faculty life and perhaps abandon some plans and goals previously set and not yet accomplished.

An important difference in daily life is the degree of autonomy experienced by faculty compared to academic leaders. Faculty typically structure their own work time and do so around their individual scholarship and teaching. Administrators usually do not structure their own time. They tend to have highly scheduled days that include a large amount of meeting time. Leaders must simultaneously handle many issues in a short amount of time; are responsible for decisions with important consequences for programs, budgets and personnel; do not have much uninterrupted individual work time; and do not have much time left over to pursue their own research agenda (Hecht, 2006; Strathe & Wilson, 2006). It is important that faculty who are considering a transition to administration are aware of the considerable change that will occur in the structure of their days, the autonomy over their schedule, the time they must be physically present in the work environment, the time outside of work hours on fund-raising, the meetings with important constituents or government representatives, and the amount of time they can devote to any one activity.

Faculty who transition to administration can expect their relationships to change. Loss of support from faculty peers is a common experience for faculty who become department chairs or deans; further, the new administrator must make evaluations and decisions about his/her former faculty peers (Hecht, 2006; Strathe & Wilson, 2006). "For some chairs changes in attitude, particularly on the part of their colleagues, comes as a cruel blow. The jokes about 'going to the dark side' are hard to brush aside when behind the humor you sense a seriousness of intent. It is not funny to be thought of as something akin to a traitor at the very moment you have accepted complex responsibilities from the noblest of motives" (Hecht, 2006, p. 7). Relationships with students, staff, and other leaders will also change accordingly (Hecht, 2006). In addition, personal relationships with family and friends likely will be affected by the change in time demands and schedule.

Department chairs and deans can experience stress from role conflict and role ambiguity (Montez et al., 2002). Role conflict results from conflicting expectations from different constituencies. "Caught between the faculty and administration, between students and faculty, or between administration and public, a dean is expected to advocate for opposing sides of issues. Invariably, a dean in such a situation must choose to perform one task at the expense of another, adding to the stress of not being able to fully meet the expectations of his or her superiors or constituents" (Montez et al., 2002, p. 244). Further, faculty who move to administration find themselves in a position between their faculty colleagues and their new allegiance to the administration.

In addition to role conflict, role ambiguity can cause stress for administrators. "Ill-defined responsibilities, mixed messages about how much authority deans actually have, unclear or unstated expectations and goals, and a lack of clarity about what is to be done and how much time should be spent doing it leave deans in a kind of leadership limbo" (Montez et al., 2002, p. 250). Role ambiguity may or may not be a factor in any given department, college, or institution.

Overall, movement into administration can change the life of a faculty member in multiple ways. In addition to the specific changes we discussed above, Gmelch and Miskin (1993) created a taxonomy of the broader role changes that occur during the transition from faculty to department chair. The nine role changes they identified from their study of beginning department chairs are as follows: from solitary to social; from focused to fragmented; from autonomy to accountability; from manuscripts to memoranda; from private to public; from professing to persuading; from stability to mobility; from client to custodian; and from austerity to prosperity (see figure 9.1).

For deans, the movement away from the faculty life continues to evolve more toward that of a corporate executive. This was demonstrated in a study by Jackson (2006), in which he compared the daily work of four deans of colleges of education to a corporate model by observing each dean for four weeks. He concluded that deans of colleges of education perform very similar roles and tasks as those of corporate executives. He further concluded that "it would be wise for incumbents and aspiring deans to develop executive skills . . . They should be very clear that they will engage in work roles for which they have no direct training [in their academic training and roles]" (p. 18). In sum, there are many factors for faculty to consider when thinking about a transition to an administrative position: the roles and responsibilities expected, the competencies required, and the lifestyle involved. This is where mentoring can be of great help.

The Transformation from Professor to Chair

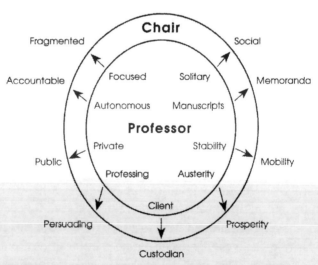

Figure 9.1.   The Transformation from Professor to Chair
From *Leadership Skills for Department Chairs* (p. 16), by W. H. Gmelch and V. D. Miskin, 1993, Bolton, MA: Anker Publishing. Reprinted with permission of first author.

*"I started out here on drums years ago, and I never dreamed
I'd wind up in a policymaking position."*

Kingman Brewster, president of Yale University, 1963–1977 (MADID #8178), and mentor to Derek Bok, president of Harvard University, 1971–1991.
Photographs of events and activities documenting Yale University, 1919-1994 (RU 690). Manuscripts and Archives, Yale University Library.

APPLICATION OF GENERAL MENTORING PRINCIPLES

The general principles of mentoring that we covered previously apply in this context as well. For example, there are many approaches one can take when mentoring faculty for a career change to administration.

Use a Variety of Mentoring Models

Because administrative leadership positions involve many new roles and competencies, mentoring relationships in this context may need to be multiple and more varied in configuration. The traditional senior-to-junior mentoring relationship remains valuable and relevant; however, other mentoring models (chapter 3) may be quite significant and may assume greater importance in the context of leadership development. For example, time-limited group mentoring in the form of discipline-specific training programs (e.g., the Association of Professors of Medicine program for new medicine department chairs), or

Derek Bok, president of Harvard University, 1971–1991
Courtesy of Special Collections Department, Harvard Law School Library.

mentoring for specific competencies (e.g., finances, conflict resolution) may be preferred over ongoing mentoring. In advanced leadership positions, peer mentoring—especially including peers outside of the home institution—may assume far greater importance than other forms of ongoing mentoring. In sum, good mentoring for leadership typically requires the use of multiple mentors, many forms of mentoring relationships, and attention to all the phases of mentoring.

Navigate the Phases of Mentoring

Once a leadership mentor has been identified, the steps we discussed in chapter 5 become applicable. The mentor should work with the mentee to set a new career vision, mission, goals, and strategies for accomplishing the goals. In addition, the mentor can help the mentee by 1) introducing the mentee to appropriate groups and networks, and 2) discussing different leadership styles to determine which amalgamation would be best suited for the mentee in the given context (Hecht, 2006).

Attend to the Mentoring Relationship

As with any mentoring situation, it is essential to build an effective relationship. In chapter 6, we discussed the following strategies for creating a relationship that is conducive for learning and growth and in which the mentee feels secure:

- Establish trust
- Communicate openly and often
- Take the initiative
- See each other as individuals
- Create and respect appropriate boundaries
- Recognize the implications of the relationship structure
- Recognize the mentee's potential challenges to success

It is especially important to recognize challenges faced by women and minorities considering leadership positions and to be mindful about using the above strategies. In academe, the barriers to women and minorities achieving major leadership positions have resulted in a leadership group that fails to reflect the demographics of either the faculty or the general population. An experienced and trusted mentor can help women and minority mentees identify ways to overcome barriers and unintended biases that could hinder their successful advancement into a leadership position.

SUMMARY

During times of actual or potential career transition, mentoring can have a tremendous impact on career development. There are many factors for faculty to consider when thinking about a transition to an administrative position: their motivation for seeking a leadership position, the roles and responsibilities expected, the competencies required, and the lifestyle involved. Mentoring is a strategy for understanding these factors and thoughtfully negotiating a successful transition.

Although the primary purpose of this book is to facilitate faculty success through mentoring, we thought it important to address the transition from faculty to administrative leadership. Higher education leaders can have significant and broad-ranging impact on their organizations. Indeed, the ability of faculty to be successful is greatly affected by the quality of leadership at their institution.

In addition, leaders who have experienced effective mentoring as either a mentor or mentee are more likely to initiate and support formal mentoring in their institution. Institution-wide mentoring programs are one of higher education's most powerful regenerative strategies. By attending to faculty vitality through mentoring, academic leaders will not only facilitate individual faculty success, but also institutional success.

Checklist for Developing, Implementing, and Assessing Mentoring Programs

Mentoring works. Participants and institutions benefit. Mentoring will continue to enrich, enliven, and affect student and faculty development now and in the future. Some chapter authors of this volume discussed their attempts to conceptualize, define, develop, implement, and assess mentoring programs in their institutions. Others provided insights into the human side of the mentoring process. While all mentoring programs have a common core of values and a commitment to help people develop their full potential and advance in educational and professional paths, *we know that there is no one way to accomplish these goals.* However, we do have sufficient evidence from the literature, research, and model programs to understand that certain basic elements must be present to make mentoring programs effective. In addition to being based on solid planning and provided with sufficient resources, mentoring programs must fit into the institutional culture, meet the needs of participants and sponsors, become integrated into the support services network, and validate and highlight their achievements.

As institutions change, as student and faculty demographics shift, as barriers to equitable advancement are broken, mentoring will evolve new goals and structures. Rather than being a definitive summary of what mentoring is or should be, the following checklist is designed to serve as a guide for those who wish to consider structured mentoring programs as an answer to the development of human resources in any institution. The checklist is not intended to be definitive or proscriptive, but instead to serve as a stimulus to asking the kind of institution-based questions necessary to launch and implement a comprehensive mentoring program.

ASSESSING INDIVIDUAL AND INSTITUTIONAL NEEDS FOR MENTORING

Why do we want a mentoring program? What specific needs will it address?

How were these needs determined (for example, by a special study, administrative mandate, identification of a problem, requests from potential users)?

Is mentoring an appropriate activity to meet these needs?

Does the institutional mission support this kind of activity?

Does the institutional development plan articulate these goals?

Do the campus climate and culture value this activity?

Are there existing programs that are potential collaborators or competitors?

Is this the right time to begin a formal program?

Are there any barriers to establishing a mentoring program?

DEFINING GOALS AND OUTCOMES FOR MENTORING

How is mentoring to be defined for your program?

Who will determine the program goals (for example, the administration, an advisory group, or the participants)?

Are these short- or long-term goals?

What are the measurable outcomes for participants?

Are there stated outcomes for the institution?

Who will determine when goals are met?

POSITIONING THE PROGRAM IN THE ORGANIZATION

Who will act as sponsors, patrons, or advocates of the program?

Which position or office will be responsible for the program?

Does this unit have sufficient power, influence, and resources to support the program?

Is mentoring to be considered an academic or a service program?

What are the implications of this decision?

Do you need an advisory committee?

What will be its role: planning, publicity, or advocacy?

Will it be a campus-wide program? A departmental program? A program for a target group (for example, minority students, women faculty, nontraditional students, new faculty, women in science, minority students in engineering, and so on)?

Will the mentoring program be part of other initiatives (for example, student counseling, faculty development, or minority programs)?

How will the program be announced and publicized?

DETERMINING AND OBTAINING PROGRAM RESOURCES

What resources are needed to accomplish program goals in terms of staff, time, space, and materials?

Who is responsible for obtaining resources? By what process?

Will resources be temporary or permanent?

Will funds come from internal or external sources?

Will there be supplemental funds from grants?

Is the program expected to generate funds?

Will an operating budget be designated for the program?

Who determines the amount of the budget and the allowable expenditures?

What staff is needed and how will it be acquired: by hiring, by loans, through volunteering, or through release time?

How much and what kind of space is required for mentoring activities?

How central and accessible is the program office for users?

DEVELOPING AND COORDINATING THE PROGRAM

How much planning time is required before the program begins for needs assessment, hiring staff, preparing materials, publicity?

Will the program follow the calendar or the academic year?

At what point will activities begin?

What activities will constitute a mentoring program: pairing mentors/mentees, mentoring groups, orientations, training sessions for participants, counseling, social activities, or tutoring?

How will the program activities be organized and scheduled?

How much structure or flexibility do you need to meet goals?

Who will be responsible for coordinating the program?

What qualifications will the coordinator need?

How much time will the coordinator give to the program?

Where will the program and coordinator be physically located?

SELECTING AND MONITORING PARTICIPANTS

How will participants be identified?

How will mentors be selected: volunteers, solicited, or referred?

How will mentors be screened: for age, ethnicity, skills, attitudes, values, gender, or what feature(s)?

What expectations will be set for participation in terms of time commitment, meetings, reports, and so on?

How will they be trained to be effective?

Will mentors be compensated or rewarded for participation?

How will mentees be selected? Will they be volunteers, will they be referred, or will they be part of special programs?

What expectations will be set for mentees?

How will mentors and mentees be matched: by age, ethnicity, gender, academic discipline, or by what other criteria?

Have you assessed the advantages and disadvantages of different kinds of matches: cross-gender, same discipline, same gender, and so on?

Who will do the matching?

Will individuals have a choice in pairing?

Will individuals have options if the match is not compatible?

Have you considered the potential problem areas in matching (for example, sexual harassment)?

How will the coordinator interact with the pairs?

Will the pairs interact with other pairs?
What will be the duration of the match?
When does the formal mentoring conclude?

ASSESSING THE PROGRAM

Why do you need to evaluate the program?
Is evaluation required for administrative support, to validate success, to obtain program data, to get feedback from participants?
When you determine the purpose for assessment, how will you choose the types of evaluation to be used?
Can you use standard methodology, or will you want to develop special forms and methods?
Do you need immediate, short-term feedback from participants?
Will this be used for program development or changes?
Do you need long-term assessment of program impact?
Do you have a plan to acquire data as the program proceeds?
Do you have the expertise to evaluate the program?
Will assessment data be available for research on the program?
Who has access to program data and for what activities?
Will you publish an annual report on the program?
What other questions and issues are crucial to your particular institution?

Developing an Academic Career Plan: Self-Assessment Questionnaire: INDIVIDUAL Factors That Promote Faculty Vitality and Career Success

For each of the following institutional vitality factors, please indicate the degree to which you agree or disagree with the statement.
(SD=Strongly Disagree, D=Disagree, A=Agree, SA=Strongly Agree)

Socialization *Understands the values, norms, expectations, and sanctions affecting established faculty.*   **SD   D   A   SA**

1. I fully understand the research, teaching, and service expectations for promotion in the appointment I hold (e.g., tenure track, nontenure track)...................................... □ □ □ □
2. I believe it is essential that a faculty member is free to conduct research in areas that may be unpopular to some groups or organizations.. □ □ □ □
3. I believe it is essential that a faculty member is free to teach topics that may be unpopular to some groups or organizations.. □ □ □ □

Personal Motivation *Driven to explore, understand, and follow one's own ideas through deliberate planning, and to advance and contribute to society through innovation, discovery, and creative works.*   **SD   D   A   SA**

1. I have a clear picture of where I want to be in my academic career in 5–7 years.. □ □ □ □
2. I have a well-defined plan for achieving my academic career goals.. □ □ □ □
3. I would describe myself as being internally driven to conduct:
   a. Research.. □ □ □ □
   b. Teaching/extension.. □ □ □ □
   c. Service/administration.. □ □ □ □

Mentoring *Beginning and mid-level members are assisted by and collaborate with established scholars.*

1. I have been (or was when I was a junior faculty member) formally assigned an advisor or mentor within my academic department:
   □ Yes   □ No—If no, skip to question 2.
   If yes, valuable guidance was provided in: **SD   D   A   SA**
   a. Research.. □ □ □ □
   b. Teaching/extension.. □ □ □ □
   c. Service/administration.. □ □ □ □
2. I have (or had when I was a junior faculty member) an "unassigned" mentor(s) either in this department or another who provided me with valuable guidance in:
   a. Research.. □ □ □ □
   b. Teaching/extension.. □ □ □ □
   c. Service/administration.. □ □ □ □

Autonomy/Commitment *Has academic freedom, plans own time and sets own goals, committed to and plays a meaningful role within the larger organization.*

	SD	D	A	SA
1. I am highly committed to contributing to the success of my:				
a. Career	☐	☐	☐	☐
b. Department	☐	☐	☐	☐
c. College	☐	☐	☐	☐
d. University	☐	☐	☐	☐
e. Discipline	☐	☐	☐	☐
2. I would like more opportunities to contribute to the leadership of my:				
a. Department	☐	☐	☐	☐
b. College	☐	☐	☐	☐
c. University	☐	☐	☐	☐
d. Discipline	☐	☐	☐	☐
3. Given my career stage, appropriate use of my knowledge/experience is being made in my:				
a. Department	☐	☐	☐	☐
b. College	☐	☐	☐	☐
c. University	☐	☐	☐	☐
d. Discipline	☐	☐	☐	☐
4. I have a high degree of input into how I wish to spend my time as a faculty member within each of my faculty roles....	☐	☐	☐	☐

In-Depth Knowledge/Skills *Familiar–within one's research/teaching area–with all major published works, projects being conducted; comfortable with study design, data collection methods, teaching skills, etc.*

	SD	D	A	SA
1. I stay very "up-to-date" on the current literature in my:				
a. Research interest area(s)	☐	☐	☐	☐
b. Teaching/extension area(s)	☐	☐	☐	☐
c. Service/administrative roles	☐	☐	☐	☐
2. I am currently up-to-date in my:				
a. Research skills (e.g., statistics, research design, data collection, lab procedure)	☐	☐	☐	☐
b. Grant-getting skills (e.g., identifying funding sources, preparing grants)	☐	☐	☐	☐
c. Education and teaching skills (curriculum design, teaching formats, evaluations)	☐	☐	☐	☐
d. Computer skills (e.g., data analysis, presentation software, web-based instruction, e-mail)	☐	☐	☐	☐
e. Writing skills (e.g., constructing concise/persuasive text and effective charts/figures)	☐	☐	☐	☐
f. Administrative skills (e.g., university procedures, personnel policies, planning)	☐	☐	☐	☐

Orientation *Committed to both external activities (e.g., regional and national meetings, collaborating with colleagues) and activities within one's organization (e.g., planning, institutional governance).*   **SD   D   A   SA**

1. I feel appreciated and valued by my local colleagues (department/college) for my work in:
   a. Research.. ☐ ☐ ☐ ☐
   b. Teaching/extension... ☐ ☐ ☐ ☐
   c. Service/administration... ☐ ☐ ☐ ☐
2. I feel appreciated and valued by my national colleagues for my work in:
   a. Research.. ☐ ☐ ☐ ☐
   b. Teaching/extension... ☐ ☐ ☐ ☐
   c. Service/administration.. ☐ ☐ ☐ ☐
3. If I were to select a faculty career again, I would choose to be:
   a. In my current discipline...................................... ☐ ☐ ☐ ☐
   b. In my current department..................................... ☐ ☐ ☐ ☐
   c. In my current college... ☐ ☐ ☐ ☐
   d. I would not choose a faculty career......................... ☐ ☐ ☐ ☐

Work Habits *Have established productive scholarly/teaching habits early in my career.*   **SD   D   A   SA**

1. I have adequate time to:
   a. Conduct research projects...................................... ☐ ☐ ☐ ☐
   b. Fulfill teaching/extension duties........................... ☐ ☐ ☐ ☐
   c. Fulfill administrative roles................................... ☐ ☐ ☐ ☐
2. I have a system that allows me to protect periods of uninterrupted time to address:
   a. Research activities.. ☐ ☐ ☐ ☐
   b. Teaching/extension activities................................ ☐ ☐ ☐ ☐
   c. Administrative activities....................................... ☐ ☐ ☐ ☐

Simultaneous Projects *Engaged in multiple, concurrent projects, so as to buffer against disillusionment if one project stalls or fails.*   **SD   D   A   SA**

1. I have more than one major research project on which I am working... ☐ ☐ ☐ ☐
2. I have significant roles in both teaching and research......... ☐ ☐ ☐ ☐

Professional Network *Members have a vibrant network of colleagues with whom they have frequent and substantive research and education communication, both impromptu and formal, in and outside of the institution.*   **SD   D   A   SA**

1. I have a well-developed network of colleagues with whom I discuss research projects and education:
   a. Within my academic department............................. ☐ ☐ ☐ ☐
   b. Outside my department/within the university.............. ☐ ☐ ☐ ☐
   c. Outside the university.. ☐ ☐ ☐ ☐

Developing an Academic Career Plan: Self-Assessment Questionnaire: INSTITUTIONAL Factors That Promote Faculty Vitality and Career Success

For each of the following institutional vitality factors, please indicate the degree to which you agree or disagree with the statement.
(SD=Strongly Disagree, D=Disagree, A=Agree, SA=Strongly Agree)

Recruitment & Selection *Great effort is expended to recruit and hire members who have the training, goals, commitment, and socialization that match the institution.*

	SD	D	A	SA
1. Effective recruitment strategies are in place for attracting the best talent in priority areas in my:				
a. Department..	☐	☐	☐	☐
b. College..	☐	☐	☐	☐

Clear Coordinating Goals *Visible, shared goals coordinate members' work.*

	SD	D	A	SA
1. There is a high expectation in my department for faculty to:				
a. Be productive in research.....................................	☐	☐	☐	☐
b. Conduct research that is externally funded..................	☐	☐	☐	☐
c. Provide quality education.....................................	☐	☐	☐	☐
2. The college has a commonly held vision for what we want to look like in the next 5 years.....................................	☐	☐	☐	☐
3. My department has a commonly held vision for what we want to look like in the next five years.........................	☐	☐	☐	☐
4. It is clear to me how my department's vision and goals are or can be related to the college's vision and goals...............	☐	☐	☐	☐
5. It is clear to me how my work and goals are or can be related to the department vision................................	☐	☐	☐	☐
6. The reward system in the department matches the departmental vision and goals....................................	☐	☐	☐	☐
7. The priorities in the department (as evidenced by such things as money allocations, new hires, cuts, etc.) match the stated vision..	☐	☐	☐	☐
8. The vision of the department is kept visible by my:				
a. Department head...	☐	☐	☐	☐
b. Division leader..	☐	☐	☐	☐
c. Departmental senior faculty.................................	☐	☐	☐	☐

Culture *Members are bonded by shared, research and teaching-related values and practices, have a safe home for testing new ideas.*

	SD	D	A	SA
1. A large portion of my academic department's faculty can be considered to:				
a. Be productive in research.....................................	☐	☐	☐	☐
b. Be significant external grant "getters"......................	☐	☐	☐	☐
c. Provide quality education.....................................	☐	☐	☐	☐
2. My department/division head is highly regarded for his/her:				
a. Research..	☐	☐	☐	☐

b. Teaching/extension.. ☐ ☐ ☐ ☐
c. Service/administration.. ☐ ☐ ☐ ☐
3. I get constructive feedback, guidance, and suggestions from my:
  a. Department head... ☐ ☐ ☐ ☐
  b. Division head.. ☐ ☐ ☐ ☐
  c. Department colleagues... ☐ ☐ ☐ ☐
  d. Colleagues outside my department.......................... ☐ ☐ ☐ ☐
  e. Dean.. ☐ ☐ ☐ ☐

Positive Group Climate *The climate is characterized by high morale, a spirit of innovation, dedication to work, receptivity to new ideas, frequent interactions, high degree of cooperation, low member turnover, good leader/member relationships, and open discussion of disagreements.*   SD   D   A   SA
1. My department head is very supportive of my efforts in:
  a. Research... ☐ ☐ ☐ ☐
  b. Teaching/extension.. ☐ ☐ ☐ ☐
  c. Service/administration.. ☐ ☐ ☐ ☐
2. My department leadership keeps us on track by clearly
  emphasizing our core missions of education and research.... ☐ ☐ ☐ ☐

Communication with Professional Network *Members have a vibrant network of colleagues with whom they have frequent and substantive (not merely social) research and education communication, both impromptu and formal, in and outside of the institution.*   SD   D   A   SA
1. I have a well-developed network of colleagues with whom I
  discuss research projects and education:
  a. Within my academic department............................. ☐ ☐ ☐ ☐
  b. Outside my department/within my university............... ☐ ☐ ☐ ☐
  c. Outside the university.. ☐ ☐ ☐ ☐

Resources *Members have access to sufficient resources such as funding, facilities, and especially humans (e.g., local peers for support, research and teaching assistants, technical consultants).*   SD   D   A   SA
1. At least weekly, I have substantive uninterrupted
  conversation with important colleagues about research and
  education in my:
  a. Department... ☐ ☐ ☐ ☐
  b. College... ☐ ☐ ☐ ☐
  c. University.. ☐ ☐ ☐ ☐
  d. Discipline.. ☐ ☐ ☐ ☐
2. I have access to adequate resources such as secretarial
  support, research/teaching assistants, computers, library
  materials, data analyses, technical support, etc., to conduct
  my:

    a. Research.. □ □ □ □
    b. Teaching/extension.. □ □ □ □
    c. Service/administration... □ □ □ □
3. My academic department provides me with, or I have from
    external or other sources, adequate support to travel to:
    a. Research-based conferences.................................... □ □ □ □
    b. Education-based conferences................................... □ □ □ □
4. I have adequate space to conduct my:
    a. Research.. □ □ □ □
    b. Teaching/extension.. □ □ □ □
    c. Service/administration... □ □ □ □
5. I have space that is well equipped for me to conduct my:
    a. Research.. □ □ □ □
    b. Teaching/extension.. □ □ □ □
    c. Service/administration... □ □ □ □

Sufficient Work Time *Members have significant periods of uninterrupted time to devote to scholarly and education activities.*   **SD D A SA**
1. I have a system that allows me to protect periods of
    uninterrupted time to conduct my:
    a. Research.. □ □ □ □
    b. Teaching/extension.. □ □ □ □
    c. Service/administration... □ □ □ □

Size/Experience/Expertise *Members offer different perspectives by virtue of differences in their degree levels, approaches to problems, and varying discipline backgrounds; the group is stable, and its size is at or above a "critical mass" a "critical mass."*   **SD D A SA**
1. The number of faculty in my department is large enough to
    accomplish our goals in:
    a. Research.. □ □ □ □
    b. Teaching/extension.. □ □ □ □
    c. Service/administration... □ □ □ □
2. The skills, expertise, and experience of the faculty in my
    department are appropriate to accomplish our goals in:
    a. Research.. □ □ □ □
    b. Teaching/extension.. □ □ □ □
    c. Service/administration... □ □ □ □

Communication *Clear and multiple forms of communication such that all members feel informed.*   **SD D A SA**
1. My department leadership (e.g., department head, senior
    faculty) make clear the expected ethical standards and
    practices in:
    a. Research.. □ □ □ □
    b. Teaching/extension.. □ □ □ □

c. Service/administration... ☐ ☐ ☐ ☐

2. My department has a communication system that allows me
to be informed in a timely fashion and adequately about
major issues, important events, and upcoming concerns....... ☐ ☐ ☐ ☐

Bishop Fellowship Program

COMPETENCIES TO FULFILL THE ROLES AND RESPONSIBILITIES OF A MEDICAL SCHOOL DEAN[a]

Leadership

1. Understands role and responsibilities of a medical school dean
2. Creates, sustains, and communicates a shared school vision
3. Facilitates and implements an effective strategic planning process for achieving vision
4. Coordinates department and center goals to collectively achieve college vision
5. Applies assertive participative leadership as a dominant leadership approach (e.g., establishing and systematically using external advisory boards and internal faculty consultative committees)
6. Understands and applies other leadership approaches as necessary
7. Identifies/enlists a core team of talented leaders who can assist in providing diverse opinions and balanced leadership for the institution—people to whom the dean can delegate with confidence
8. Motivates, inspires, and persuades through personal efforts (e.g., notes, phone calls) and structural mechanisms, such as creating merit systems and new appointment types

---

[a]The underlying implication for the action competencies is an in-depth understanding about each of them. For example, "creates, sustains, and communicates a shared school vision" implies you understand the importance of and how to develop a shared vision.

9. Establishes and effectively uses the governance systems and policies of the university and school
10. Establishes an effective practice plan
11. Effectively works within institutional personnel policies (e.g., recruiting, hiring, laying off, benefits)
12. Effectively works with institutional personnel groups (e.g., faculty, staff, collective bargaining units)
13. Implements ways to help faculty, administrators, and staff continually improve, such as sabbaticals, leaves, workshops, coaching, seminars, collaborative teaching, and professional meetings
14. Promotes creative, innovative, resourceful entrepreneurial activities through personal efforts and structural ones (e.g., establishing special units to facilitate private partnerships, subcommittees of the advisory board, incentives)
15. Ensures adequate facilities and support staff for education, research, and patient care
16. Understands the external and local environment and critical issues that impact the school and acts to abrogate negative impacts and capitalize on positive ones
17. Applies organizational change strategies, as appropriate
18. Has a commitment to and understands how to promote the success of all college members, especially people of color, women, and senior members
19. Provides opportunities for others to advance with leadership
20. Provides service to the university and external constituencies (e.g., participates in task forces and search committees)
21. Effectively follows procedures and ensures compliance to regulations in regard to personnel (e.g., hiring, evaluation, terminating, harassment) and education (e.g., admissions, evaluation)

Recruitment

22. Effectively recruits department heads and faculty who are best suited to help achieve the school vision
23. Seeks diversity in department heads and faculty

Finances

24. Understands financing, revenues, and expenses of medical school
25. Conducts fund-raising within institutional guidelines with, for example, industry, individuals, foundations, and legislatures
26. Develops a budget that furthers the vision
27. Understands management and display of finances
28. Understands investments
29. Understands short-term and long-term management of physical plant

Relationships/Partnerships

30. Understands issues in hospital and physician reimbursement
31. Develops relationships with key external influential people and networks that can provide support (e.g., other medical school deans, professional association officers)
32. Facilitates interdisciplinary activity within the college and with other colleges
33. Develops relationships with key internal players that can provide support and networks (e.g., the person to whom you report, the president, the regents, the state and U.S. legislature, professional organizations, deans of other schools)
34. Works effectively in the political and regulatory environments

Education

35. Facilitates curriculum that matches school vision and prepares learners to succeed
36. Oversees academic quality of residency and fellowship education
37. Understands appropriate and effective strategies to recruit students, residents, and fellows
38. Changes medical school curriculum to match the advances in science, curriculum design, teaching, evaluation, and the needs of society
39. Understands ethics regarding education

40. Understands financial aid
41. Understands regulations and accreditation requirements for the school
42. Understands funding mechanisms for education

Research

43. Strategically recruits faculty and fundraises to facilitate research that advances science, matches the school's vision, and encourages interdisciplinary work
44. Understands regulations regarding research
45. Understands ethics regarding research
46. Understands funding mechanisms for research

Clinical

47. Understands the management and interrelations of clinical operations (e.g., clinics, practice plans, teaching hospitals)
48. Understands the economics of health-care delivery
49. Understands the relationships and affiliations with university and community teaching hospitals
50. Understands the ethics of patient care
51. Understands the regulations regarding patient care
52. Ensures patient care quality and clinical competence

Culture and Communication

53. Demonstrates good character (integrity, honesty, trustworthiness, ethical behavior)
54. Is able to articulate as well as demonstrate knowledge of and regard for the values of higher education institutions—including quality education and research, academic freedom and tenure, and consultative and joint governance
55. Establishes a sense of community and common goals
56. Maintains an atmosphere in which faculty experience a sense of institutional pride

57. Communicates effectively through listening, speaking, writing, and public presentation, including the media
58. Applies interpersonal skills (e.g., empathy, sensitivity, rapport-building)
59. Anticipates, negotiates, and manages conflict, problems, and stressful and changing situations
60. Responds in a timely way

Management Skills

61. Effectively organizes, plans, delegates, and prioritizes work
62. Knows how to lead and manage groups, teams, committees, projects, and meetings
63. Evaluates individual and organizational effectiveness
64. Identifies which decisions need immediate action and which do not; makes appropriate, timely, and thoughtful decisions; uses good judgment
65. Demonstrates knowledge of the college/university, as well as relevant state and U.S. government policies, procedures, and practices
66. Understands and introduces technology applications
67. Can handle back-to-back meetings and loss of calendar control
68. Manages crises
69. Can manage conflict

Personal Characteristics

70. understands the personal characteristics of successful academic leaders such as: enjoys promoting the success of others rather than self; gets excited about working for the collective good; engenders trust in others, even those with whom one disagrees; is consistent on positions, commitments, and promises—across constituencies; works effectively with (even enjoys) unique and perhaps stubborn and narrow-minded people; engenders the belief among others, especially subordinates, that their concerns and success are important; enjoys managing and solving multiple tasks; can work long hours

71. Understands how well one's own characteristics match with those of successful academic leaders

Career Management

72. Effectively manages career

Note. The Bishop Fellowship is a one-year program which identifies and develops qualified senior family medicine faculty to successfully assume positions of greater responsibility in academic medicine. The program includes the use of projects, mentorships with current deans or vice presidents, and formal educational programs. For more information go to http://www.stfm.org/foundation/bishop.htm.

Works Cited

Abbott, I. O. (2000). *The lawyer's guide to mentoring*. Washington, DC: National Association for Law Placement.

Abbott, I. O. (2006). Mentoring groups and mentoring circles: The need for careful planning. [Electronic Entry] *Management Solutions, 15* (summer). Retrieved February 15, 2007, from http://www.idaabbott.com/news/news15.html.

Acker, S., & Armenti, C. (2004). Sleepless in academia. *Gender and Education, 16*(1), 3–24.

Allen, T. D., Eby, L. T., Poteet, M. L., Lentz, E., & Lima, L. (2004). Career benefits associated with mentoring for protégés: A meta-analysis. *Journal of Applied Psychology, 89*(1), 127–136.

Allen, T. D., Lentz, E., & Day, R. (2006). Career success outcomes associated with mentoring others: A comparison of mentors and non-mentors. *Journal of Career Development, 32*(3), 272–285.

Allen, T. D., Poteet, M. L., & Burroughs, S. M. (1997). The mentor's perspective: A qualitative inquiry and future research agenda. *Journal of Vocational Behavior, 51*(1), 70–89.

Ambrose, S., Huston, T., & Norman, M. (2005). A qualitative method for assessing faculty satisfaction. *Research in Higher Education, 46*(7), 803–830.

American Association for Higher Education Task Force on Professional Growth (1984). *Vitality without mobility: The faculty opportunities audit* (Current Issues in Higher Education No. 4). Washington, DC: American Association for Higher Education.

Aran, L., & Ben-David, J. (1968). Socialization and career patterns as determinants of productivity of medical researchers. *Journal of Health and Social Behavior, 9*, 3–15.

August, L., & Waltman, J. (2004). Culture, climate, and contribution: Career satisfaction among female faculty. *Research in Higher Education*, *45*(2), 177–192.

Bakken, L. L. (2005). Who are physician-scientists' role models? Gender makes a difference. *Academic Medicine*, *80*(5), 502–506.

Bakken, L. L., Sheridan, J., & Carnes, M. (2003). Gender differences among physician-scientists in self-assessed abilities to perform clinical research. *Academic Medicine*, *78*(12), 1281–1286.

Baldwin, R. G., Lunceford, C. J., & Vanderlinden, K. E. (2005). Faculty in the middle years: Illuminating an overlooked phase of academic life. *Review of Higher Education*, *29*(1), 97–118.

Barnes, L. L. B., Agago, M. O., & Coombs, W. T. (1998). Effects of job-related stress on faculty intention to leave academia. *Research in Higher Education*, *39*(4), 457-469.

Bartunek, J. M., Kram, K. E., Coffey, R., Lenn, D. J., Moch, M. K., & O'Neill, H. (1997). A group mentoring journey into the department chair role. *Journal of Management Inquiry*, *6*(4), 270–279.

Belker, J. S. (1985). The education of mid-career professors: Is it continuing? *College Teaching*, *33*(2), 68–71.

Berberet, J., Brown, B. E., Bland, C. J., Risbey, K. R., & Trotman, C. (2005). Planning for the generational turnover of the faculty: Faculty perceptions and institutional practices. In R. Clark & J. Ma (Eds.), *Recruitment, retention, and retirement in higher education: Building and managing the faculty of the future* (pp. 80–100). Northampton, MA: Edward Elgar Publishing.

Bickel, J., Wara, D., Atkinson, B. F., Cohen, L. S., Dunn, M., Hostler, S. et al. (2002). Increasing women's leadership in academic medicine: Report of the AAMC Project Implementation Committee. *Academic Medicine*, *77*(10), 1043–1061.

Bickel, J., & Brown, A. J. (2005). Generation X: Implications for faculty recruitment and development in academic health centers. *Academic Medicine*, *80*(3), 205–210.

Blackburn, R. T. (1979). Academic careers: Patterns and possibilities. *Current Issues in Higher Education*, *2*, 25–27.

Blackburn, R. T., & Fox, T. J. (1976). The socialization of a medical school faculty. *Journal of Medical Education*, *51*(10), 806–817.

Bland, C. J., & Bergquist, W. H. (1997). *The vitality of senior faculty members: Snow on the roof—fire in the furnace. ASHE-ERIC Higher Education Report*, *25*(7). Washington, DC: George Washington University, Graduate School of Education and Human Development.

Bland, C. J., Center, B. A., Finstad, D. A., Risbey, K. R., & Staples, J. G. (2005). A theoretical, practical, predictive model of faculty and department research productivity. *Academic Medicine, 80*(3), 225–237.

Bland, C. J., Hitchcock, M. A., Anderson, W. A., & Stritter, F. T. (1987). Faculty development fellowship programs in family medicine. *Journal of Medical Education, 62*(August), 632–641.

Bland, C. J., & Risbey, K. R. (2006). Faculty development programs. *Effective Practices for Academic Leaders* (Stylus Publishing, L.L.C.), *1*(7), 1–16.

Bland, C. J., & Ruffin, M. T., IV. (1992). Characteristics of a productive research environment: Literature review. *Academic Medicine, 67*(6), 385–397.

Bland, C. J., & Schmitz, C. C. (1986). Characteristics of the successful researcher and implications for faculty development. *Journal of Medical Education, 61*, 22–31.

Bland, C. J., Schmitz, C. C., Stritter, F. T., Aluise, J. A., Henry, R. C. (1988). Project to identify essential faculty skills and develop model curricula for faculty development programs. *Journal of Medical Education, 63*, 467–469.

Bland, C. J., Schmitz, C. C., Stritter, F. T., Henry, R. C., & Aluise, J. A. (1990). *Successful faculty in academic medicine: Essential skills and how to acquire them.* New York: Springer Publishing.

Bland, C. J., Seaquist, E., Pacala, J. T., Center, B., & Finstad, D. (2002). One school's strategy to assess and improve the vitality of its faculty. *Academic Medicine, 77*(5), 368–376.

Bland, C. J., Weber-Main, A. M., Lund, S. M., & Finstad, D. A. (2005). *The research-productive department: Strategies from departments that excel.* Bolton, MA: Anker Publishing Co.

Blau, J. R. (1976). Scientific recognition: Academic context and professional role. *Social Studies of Science, 6*, 533–545.

Bogdewic, S. (1986). Advancement and promotion: Managing the individual career. In W. C. McGaghie, & J. J. Frey (Eds.), *Handbook for the academic physician* (pp. 22–36). New York: Springer-Verlag.

Bova, B., & Kroth, M. (1999). Closing the gap: The mentoring of Generation X. *Journal of Adult Education, 27*(1), 7–17.

Bova, B., & Kroth, M. (2001). Workplace learning and Generation X. *Journal of Workplace Learning, 13*(2), 57–65.

Bower, D. J., Diehr, S., Morzinski, J. A., & Simpson, D. E. (1998). Support-challenge-vision: A model for faculty mentoring. *Medical Teacher, 20*(6), 595–597.

Bower, D. J., Diehr, S., Morzinski, J. A., & Simpson, D. E. (1999). *Mentoring guidebook for academic physicians: Using support. challenge and vision to guide colleagues toward academic success.* Milwaukee: Center for Ambulatory Teaching Excellence, Department of Family and Community Medicine, Medical College of Wisconsin.

Bowman, S. R., Kite, M. E., Branscombe, N. R., & Williams, S. (1999). Developmental relationships of Black Americans in the academy. In A. J. Murrell, F. J. Crosby, & R. J. Ely (Eds.), *Mentoring dilemmas: Developmental relationships within multicultural organizations* (pp. 21–46). Mahwah, NJ: Lawrence Erlbaum Associates.

Boyle, M. (2005). Most mentoring programs stink—but yours doesn't have to. *Training, August,* 12–15.

Boyle, P., & Boice, B. (1998). Systematic mentoring for new faculty teachers and graduate teaching assistants. *Innovative Higher Education, 22*(3), 157–179.

Brinson, J. A., & Kottler, J. (1993). Cross-cultural mentoring in counselor education: A strategy for retaining minority faculty. *Counselor Education and Supervision, 32*(4), 241–253.

Bucher, R., & Stelling, J. G. (1977). *Becoming professional.* Beverly Hills, CA: Sage Publications.

Byrne, M. W., & Keefe, M. R. (2002). Building research competence in nursing through mentoring. *Journal of Nursing Scholarship, 34*(4), 391–396.

Caffarella, R. S., Armour, R. A., Fuhrmann, B. S., & Wergin, J. F. (1989). Mid-career faculty: Refocusing the perspective. *Review of Higher Education, 12*(4), 403–410.

Caffarella, R. S., & Zinn, L. F. (1999). Professional development for faculty: A conceptual framework of barriers and supports. *Innovative Higher Education, 23*(4), 241–254.

Caffrey, J. (1969). Predictions for higher education in the 1970's. In J. Caffrey (Ed.), *The future academic community: Continuity and change.* Washington, DC: American Council on Education.

Cameron, S. W., & Blackburn, R. T. (1981). Sponsorship and academic career success. *Journal of Higher Education, 52*(4), 369–377.

Carnes, M., Geller, S., Fine, E., Sheridan, J., & Handelsman, J. (2005). NIH Director's Pioneer Awards: Could the selection process be biased against women? *Journal of Women's Health, 14*(8), 684–691.

Carr, R. (2000). *A chart summarizing four different types of mentoring: Intentional, traditional, peer, and transition.* Victoria, BC: Peer Systems Consulting Group. [Electronic Entry] Retrieved September 10, 2006, from http://www.mentors.ca/Peer_Resources_Network.html/Projects

Carr, P. L., Ash, A. S., Friedman, R. H., Scaramucci, A., Barnett, R. C., Szala-cha, L., et al. (1998). Relation of family responsibilities and gender to the productivity and career satisfaction of medical faculty. *Annals of Internal Medicine, 129*(7), 532–538.

Carr, P. L., Bickel, J., & Inui, T. S. (Eds.) (2004). *Taking root in a forest clearing: A resource guide for medical faculty.* Boston: Boston University School of Medicine.

Carroll, J. B., & Gmelch, W. H. (1994). Department chair's perceptions of the importance of their duties. *Journal of Higher Education Management, 10*(1): 49–63.

Clark, S. M., & Corcoran, M. (1986). Perspectives on the professional social-ization of women faculty. *Journal of Higher Education, 57*(1), 20–43.

Clark, S. M., & Lewis, D. R. (1985). *Faculty vitality and institutional pro-ductivity: Critical perspectives for higher education.* New York: Teachers College Press.

Clawson, J. G., & Kram, K. E. (1984). Managing cross-gender mentoring. *Business Horizons, 27*(3), 22–32.

Conway, M. E., & Glass, L. K. (1978). Socialization for survival in the aca-demic world. *Nursing Outlook, 26*(7), 424–429.

Corcoran, M., & Clark, S. M. (1984). Professional socialization and contem-porary career attitudes of three faculty generations. *Research in Higher Education, 20*(2), 131–153.

Cox, T. H., Lobel, S. A., & McLeod, P. L. (1991). Effects of ethnic group cultural differences on cooperative and competitive behavior on a group task. *Academy of Management Journal, 34*(4), 827–847.

Creswell, J. W. (1986). Concluding thoughts: Observing, promoting, evaluat-ing, and reviewing research performance. In J. W. Creswell (Ed.), *Mea-suring faculty research performance* (New Directions for Institutional Research, No. 50, pp. 87–102). San Francisco: Jossey-Bass.

Creswell, J. W., Wheeler, D. W., Seagren, A. T., Egly, N. J., & Beyer, K. D. (1990). *The academic chairperson's handbook.* Lincoln: University of Nebraska Press.

Curtis, P., Dickinson, P., Steiner, J., Lanphear, B., & Vu, K. (2003). Building capacity for research in family medicine: Is the blueprint faulty? *Family Medicine, 35*(2), 124–130.

Daloz, L. (1999). *Mentor: Guiding the journey of adult learners.* San Fran-cisco: Jossey-Bass.

Demmy, T. L., Kivlahan, C., & Stone, T. T. (2002). Physicians' perceptions of institutional and leadership factors influencing their job satisfaction at one academic medical center. *Academic Medicine, 77*, 1235–1240.

Diehl, P. F., & Simpson, R. D. (1989). Investing in junior faculty: The teaching improvement program (TIPs). *Innovative Higher Education, 13*(2), 147–157.

Dill, D. D. (1986). Local barriers and facilitators of research. Paper presented at the 1986 Annual Meeting of the American Educational Research Association, San Francisco.

Dixon, M. N. (2006). Peer-to-peer leadership development. *Harvard Business Review*, 56–57.

Dohm, F. A., & Cummings, W. (2002). Research mentoring and women in clinical psychology. *Psychology of Women Quarterly, 26*(2), 163–167.

Drotar, D., & Avner, E. D. (2003). Critical choices in mentoring the next generation of academic pediatricians: Nine circles of hell or salvation? *Journal of Pediatrics, 142*(1), 1–2.

Dubin, R. (Ed.). (1976). *Handbook of work. organization. and society.* Chicago: Rand McNally College Publishing Co.

Dundar, H., & Lewis, D. R. (1998). Determinants of research productivity in higher education. *Research in Higher Education, 39*(6), 607–631.

Duderstadt, J. J. (2001). Leading higher education in an era of rapid change. University of Michigan Millennium Project. [Electronic Entry] Retrieved June 15, 2006, from http://milproj.ummu.umich.edu/publications/midwest_higher_ed/download/ midwest_higher_ed.pdf

Ehrich, L. C., Hansford, B., & Tennent, L. (2004). Formal mentoring programs in education and other professions: A review of the literature. *Educational Administration Quarterly, 40*(4), 518–540.

Erkut, S., & Mokros, J. R. (1984). Professors as models and mentors for college students. *American Educational Research Journal, 21*, 399–417.

Ernst & Young (2007). About Ernst & Young. [Electronic Entry] Retrieved July 5, 2007, from http://www.ey.com/global/content.nsf/International/About_EY

Etzkowitz, H., Kemelgor, C., & Uzzi, B. (2000). *Athena Unbound: The Advancement of Women in Science and Technology.* Cambridge, England: Cambridge University Press.

Field, M. B. (2006). Mentors and protégés: What protégés bring to the equation. *Faculty Vitae.* [Electronic Entry] Retrieved December 11, 2006, from http://www.aamc.org/members/facultydev/facultyvitae/fall06/lesson.htm

Finkelstein, M. J. (1996). Faculty vitality in higher education. In *Integrating research on faculty: Seeking new ways to communicate about the academic life of faculty.* Conference report: Results of a forum sponsored by the National Center for Education Statistics, The Association for Institutional Research, and the American Association of State Colleges and Universities,

January 10–11, 1994 (pp. 71–80). Washington, DC: U.S. Department of Education, National Center for Education Statistics NCES 96 849.

Fox, M. F. (1991). Gender, environmental milieu, and productivity in science. In H. Zuckerman, J. R. Cote, & J. T. Bruer (Eds.), *The outer circle: Women in the scientific community* (pp. 188–204). New York: W.W. Norton.

Gmelch, W. H., & Miskin, V. (1993). *Leadership skills for department chairs.* Bolton, MA: Anker Publishing.

Goodwin, L. D., Stevens, E. A., & Bellamy, G. T. (1998). Mentoring among faculty in schools, colleges, and departments of education. *Journal of Teacher Education, 49*(5), 334–343.

Goto, S. (1999). Asian Americans and developmental relationships. In A. J. Murrell, F. J. Crosby, & R. J. Ely (Eds.), *Mentoring dilemmas: Developmental relationships within multicultural organizations* (pp. 47–62). Mahwah, NJ: Lawrence Erlbaum Associates.

Greenhaus, J. H., & Parasuraman, S. (1993). Job performance attributions and career advancement prospects: An examination of gender and race effects. *Organizational Behavior and Human Decision Processes, 55*(2), 273–297.

Hazzard, W. R. (1999). Mentoring across the professional lifespan in academic geriatrics. *Journal of the American Geriatrics Society, 47*(12), 1466–1470.

Hecht, I. W. D. (2006). Becoming a department chair: To be or not to be? *Effective Practices for Academic Leaders, 1*(3), 1–16.

Heilman, M. E., Wallen, A. S., Fuchs, D., & Tamkins, M. M. (2004). Penalties for success: Reactions to women who succeed at male gender-typed tasks. *Journal of Applied Psychology, 89*(3), 416–427.

Hezlett, S. A., & Gibson, S. K. (2005). Mentoring and human resource development: Where we are and where we need to go. *Advances in Developing Human Resources, 7*(4), 446–469.

Higgins, M. C., & Thomas, D. A. (2001). Constellations and careers: Toward understanding the effects of multiple developmental relationships. *Journal of Organizational Behavior, 22*(3), 223–247.

Hitchcock, M. A., Bland, C. J., Hekelman, F. P., & Blumenthal, M. G. (1995). Professional networks: The influence of colleagues on the academic success of faculty. *Academic Medicine, 70*(12), 1108–1116.

Hobbs, B. K., Weeks, H. S., & Finch, J. H. (2005). Estimating the mark-to-market premium required to fill vacant business school faculty lines: The case of finance. *Journal of Education for Business, May/June,* 253–258.

Jackson, J. E. L. (2006). The nature of academic dean's work: Moving toward an academic executive behavior model in higher education. *Journal of the Professoriate, 1,* 7–22.

Johnson-Bailey, J., & Cervero, R. M. (2002). Cross-cultural mentoring as a context for learning. *New Directions for Adult and Continuing Education*, *96*, 15–26.

Johnsrud, L. K., & Des Jarlais, C. D. (1994). Barriers to tenure for women and minorities. *The Review of Higher Education*, *17*(4), 335–353.

Johnsrud, L. K., & Heck, R. H. (1994). A university's faculty: Identifying who will leave and who will stay. *Journal for Higher Education Management*, *10*(1), 71–84.

Johnsrud, L. K., & Sadao, K. C. (1998). The common experience of "Otherness": Ethnic and racial minority faculty. *The Review of Higher Education*, *21*(4), 315–342.

Karpiak, I. E. (1996). Ghosts in a wilderness: Problems and priorities of faculty at mid-career and mid-life. *The Canadian Journal of Higher Education*, *26*(3), 49–78.

Kelly, M. E. (1986). Enablers and inhibitors to research productivity among high and low producing vocational education faculty members. *Journal of Vocational Education Research*, *11*(4), 63–80.

Kember, D., & Leung, D. Y. P. (2006). Characterising a teaching and learning environment conducive to making demands on students while not making their workload excessive. *Studies in Higher Education*, *31*(2), 185–198.

Kemelgor, C., & Etzkowitz, H. (2001). Overcoming isolation: Women's dilemmas in American academic science. *Minerva: A Review of Science, Learning and Policy*, *39*(2), 239–257.

Konrad, A. M. (1991). Faculty productivity and demographics. *Thought and Action*, *7*(2), 19–54.

Kram, K. E. (1985). *Mentoring at work: Developmental relationships in organizational life*. Glenview, IL: Scott Foresman and Company.

Kram, K. E., & Isabella, L. A. (1985). Mentoring alternatives: The role of peer relationships in career development. *Academy of Management Journal*, *28*(1), 110–132.

Lancaster, L. C., & Stillman, D. (2002). *When generations collide: Who they are. Why they clash. How to solve the generational puzzle at work*. New York: HarperCollins.

Levinson, D. J. (1986). A conception of adult development. *American Psychologist*, *41*(1), 3–13.

Levinson, W., Kaufman, K., Clark, B., & Tolle, S. W. (1991). Mentors and role models for women in academic medicine. *Western Journal of Medicine*, *154*(4), 423–426.

Lewis-Stevenson, S., Hueston, W. J., Mainous, A. G., III, Bazell, C., & Ye, X. (2001). Female and underrepresented minority faculty in academic departments of family medicine: Are women and minorities better off in family medicine? *Family Medicine, 33*(6), 459–465.

Liu, M., & Mallon, W. T. (2004). Tenure in transition: Trends in basic science faculty appointment policies at U.S. medical schools. *Academic Medicine, 79*(3), 205–213.

Long, J. (1997). The dark side of mentoring. *Australian Educational Research, 24*(2), 115–123.

Long, J. S., & McGinnis, R. (1981). Organizational context and scientific productivity. *American Sociological Review, 46*, 422–442.

Lorsch, J. W., & Tierney, T. J. (2002). *Aligning the stars: How to succeed when professionals drive results.* Boston: Harvard Business School Publishing.

Manger, T., & Eikeland, O. (1990). Factors predicting staff's intentions to leave the university. *Higher Education, 19*, 281–291.

Martell, R. F. (1991). Sex bias at work: The effects of attentional and memory demands on performance ratings of men and women. *Journal of Applied Social Psychology, 21*(23), 1939–1960.

Martin, C. A., & Tulgan, B. (2001). *Managing Generation Y: Global citizens born in the late seventies and early eighties.* Amherst, MA: HRD Press.

Martin, C. A., & Tulgan, B. (2002). *Managing the generation mix: From collision to collaboration.* Amherst, MA: HRD Press.

Mason, M. A., & Goulden, M. (2002). Do babies matter? The effect of family formation on the lifelong careers of academic men and women. *Academe, 88*(6), 21–27.

Mason, M. A., & Goulden, M. (2004a). Do babies matter (Part II): Closing the baby gap. *Academe, 90*(6), 11–15.

Mason, M. A., & Goulden, M. (2004b). Marriage and baby blues: Redefining gender equity in the academy. *Annals of the American Academy of Political and Social Science, 596*(November), 86–103.

Matier, M. W. (1990). Retaining faculty: A tale of two campuses. *Research in Higher Education, 31*(1), 39–61.

McCormick, T. (1991, April). An analysis of some pitfalls of traditional mentoring for minorities and women in higher education. Paper presented at the Annual Meeting of the American Education Research Association, Chicago.

McGee, G. W., & Ford, R. C. (1987). Faculty research productivity and intention to change positions. *The Review of Higher Education, 11*(autumn), 1–16.

Melicher, R. (2000). The perceived value of research and teaching mentoring by finance academicians. *Financial Practice and Education* (spring/summer), 166–174.

Menges, R. J., & Exum, W. H. (1983). Barriers to the progress of women and minority faculty. *Journal of Higher Education, 54*(2), 123–144.

Mervis, J. (2005). Six women among 13 NIH 'Pioneers.' *Science, 309*(5744), 2149.

Mills, O. F., Zyzanski, S. J., & Flocke, S. (1995). Factors associated with research productivity in family practice residencies. *Family Medicine, 27*(3), 188–193.

Moe, M., & Blodget, H. (2000). *The knowledge web: People power—fuel for the new economy.* New York: Merrill Lynch & Co., Global Securities Research & Economics Group, Global Fundamental Equity Research Department.

Montez, J. M., Wolverton, M., & Gmelch, W. H. (2002). The roles and challenges of deans. *The Review of Higher Education, 26*(2), 241–266.

Mortimer, J. T., & Simmons, R. G. (1978). Adult socialization. *Annual Review of Sociology, 4,* 421–454.

Morzinski, J. A., Diehr, S., Bower, D. J., & Simpson, D. E. (1996). A descriptive, cross-sectional study of formal mentoring for faculty. *Family Medicine, 28*(6), 434–438.

Mundt, M. H. (2001). An external mentor program: Stimulus for faculty research development. *Journal of Professional Nursing, 17*(1), 40–45.

Noe, R. A. (1988). Women and mentoring: A review and research agenda. *Academy of Management Review, 13*(1), 65–78.

Nunez-Smith, M., Curry, L. A., Bigby, J., Berg, D., Krumholz, H. M., & Bradley, E. H. (2007). Impact of race on the professional lives of physicians of African descent. *Annals of Internal Medicine, 146*(1), 45–51.

Nyre, G. F., & Reilly, K. C. (1979). *Professional education in the eighties: Challenges and responses. AAHE-ERIC Higher Education Research Report No. 8.* Washington, DC: American Association for Higher Education.

Olsen, D., Maple, S. A., & Stage, F. K. (1995). Women and minority faculty job satisfaction: Professional role interests, professional satisfactions, and institutional fit. *The Journal of Higher Education, 66*(3), 267–293.

Padilla, A. M. (1994). Ethnic minority scholars, research, and mentoring: Current and future issues. *Educational Researcher, 23*(4), 24–27.

Paul, S., Stein, F., Ottenbacher, K. J., & Liu, Y. (2002). The role of mentoring on research productivity among occupational therapy faculty. *Occupational Therapy International, 9*(1), 24–40.

Pellino, G. R., Boberg, A. L., Blackburn, R. T., & O'Connell, C. (1981). *Planning and evaluating professional growth programs for faculty.* East

Lansing: Center for the Study of Higher Education, School of Education, University of Michigan.

Peluchette, J. V., & Jeanquart, S. (2000). Professionals' use of different mentor sources at various career stages: Implications for career success. *Journal of Social Psychology, 140*(5), 549–564.

Pelz, D. C., & Andrews, F. M. (1966). *Scientists in organizations: Productive climates for research and development.* New York: John Wiley & Sons.

Perkoff, G. T. (1985). The research environment in family practice. *Journal of Family Practice, 21*(5), 389–393.

Perry, R. P., Clifton, R. A., Menec, V. H., Struthers, C. W., & Menges, R. J. (2000). Faculty in transition: A longitudinal analysis of perceived control and type of institution in the research productivity of newly hired faculty. *Research in Higher Education, 41*(2), 165–194.

Pierce, G. (1998). Developing new university faculty through mentoring. *Journal of Humanistic Education & Development, 37*(1), 27–38.

Pololi, L. H., Knight, S. M., Dennis, K., & Frankel, R. M. (2002). Helping medical school faculty realize their dreams: An innovative, collaborative mentoring program. *Academic Medicine, 77*(5), 377–384.

Pololi, L., & Knight, S. (2005). Mentoring faculty in academic medicine: A new paradigm. *Journal of General Internal Medicine, 20*(9), 866–870.

Ragins, B. R. (1997). Diversified mentoring relationships in organizations: A power perspective. *Academy of Management Review, 22*(2), 482–521.

Ragins, B. R., & Cotton, J. L. (1991). Easier said than done: Gender differences in perceived barriers to gaining a mentor. *Academy of Management Journal, 34*(4), 939–951.

Ragins, B. R., & Cotton, J. L. (1993). Gender and willingness to mentor in organizations. *Journal of Management, 19*(1), 97–111.

Ragins, B. R., Cotton, J. L., & Miller, J. S. (2000). Marginal mentoring: The effects of type of mentor, quality of relationship, and program design on work and career attitudes. *The Academy of Management Journal, 43*(6), 1177–1194.

Ragins, B. R., & McFarlin, D. B. (1990). Perceptions of mentor roles in cross-gender mentoring relationships. *Journal of Vocational Behavior, 37*, 321–339.

Ragins, B. R., & Scandura, T. A. (1994). Gender differences in expected outcomes of mentoring relationships. *Academy of Management Journal, 37*(4), 957–971.

Ragins, B. R., & Scandura, T. A. (1999). Burden or blessing? Expected costs and benefits of being a mentor. *Journal of Organizational Behavior, 20*, 493–509.

Raines, C. (2003). *Connecting generations: The sourcebook for a new workplace*. Menlo Park, CA: Crisp Publications.

Rausch, D. K., Ortiz, B. P., Douthitt, R. A., & Reed, L. L. (1989). The academic revolving door: Why do women get caught? *CUPA Journal, 40*(1), 1–16.

Rice, E. R. (1983, April). Being professional academically. In Dan T. Bedloe (Ed.), *Critical aspects of faculty development programs. Proceedings of the Invitational Seminar on Faculty Development*. Sherman, TX: ERIC ED 238 387.

Rice, E. R., Sorcinelli, M. D., Deane, M., & Austin, A. E. (2000). *Heeding new voices: Academic careers for a new generation (Inquiry Number 7)*. Working Paper Series. New Pathways: Faculty Careers and Employment for the 21st Century. (ERIC Document Reproduction Service No. ED346082). Washington, DC: American Association of Higher Education.

Ritchie, A., & Genoni, P. (2002). Group mentoring and professionalism: A programme evaluation. *Library Management, 23*(1/2), 68–78.

Roberts, K. (1997). Nurse academics' scholarly productivity: Framed by the system, facilitated by mentoring. *Australian Journal of Advanced Nursing, 14*(3), 5–14.

Robinson, J. D. & Cannon, D. L. (2005). Mentoring in the academic medical setting: The gender gap. *Journal of Clinical Psychology in Medical Settings, 12*(3), 265–270.

Rolfe, A. (2006). How to design and run your own mentoring program: Mentoring works! In *Mentoring works*. [Electronic Entry] Retrieved February 21, 2007, from www.mentoring-works.com

Rosener, J. B. (1990). Ways women lead. *Harvard Business Review, 68*(6), 119–125.

Rosser, V. J. (2004). Faculty members' intentions to leave: A national study of their worklife and satisfaction. *Research in Higher Education, 45*(3), 285–309.

Rothblum, E. D. (1988). Leaving the ivory tower: Factors contributing to women's voluntary resignation from academia. *Frontiers, 10*(2), 14–17.

Scandura, T. A. (1998). Dysfunctional mentoring relationships and outcomes. *Journal of Management, 24*(3), 449–467.

Seldin, P. (2006). Tailoring faculty development programs to faculty career stages. In S. Chadwick-Blossey & D. R. Robertson (Eds.), *To improve the academy: Resources for faculty. institutional and organizational development* (Vol. 24, pp. 137–146). Bolton, MA: Anker Publishing.

Seymour, E. (1995). The loss of women from science, mathematics, and engineering undergraduate majors: An explanatory account. *Science Education, 79*(4), 437–473.

Shea, G. F. (1999). *Crisp: Making the most of being mentored: How to grow from a mentoring partnership (Fifty Minutes Series)*. Boston: NETg, a division of Thomson Learning.

Sindermann, C. J. (1985). *The joy of science: Excellence and its rewards*. New York: Plenum Press.

Smart, J. C. (1990). A causal model of faculty turnover intentions. *Research in Higher Education, 31*(5), 405–424.

Sorcinelli, M. D. (1988). Satisfactions and concerns of new university teachers. In L. Kurfiss, L. Hilsen, S. Kahn, M. D. Sorcinelli, & R. Tiberius (Eds.), *To improve the academy: Resources for student. faculty. and institutional development* (Vol. 7, pp. 121–133). Stillwater, OK: New Forums Press.

Sorcinelli, M. D. (1992). New and junior faculty stress: Research and responses. In M. D. Sorcinelli & A. E. Austin (Eds.), *Developing new and junior faculty* (New Directions for Teaching and Learning, No. 50, pp. 27–37). San Francisco: Jossey-Bass.

Sorcinelli, M. D. (1994). Effective approaches to new faculty development. *Journal of Counseling & Development, 72*(5), 474–479.

Soto-Greene, M. L., Sanchez, J., Churrango, J., & Salas-Lopez, D. (2005). Latino faculty development in U.S. medical schools: A Hispanic Center of Excellence perspective. *Journal of Hispanic Higher Education, 4*(4), 366–376.

Steele, B. (2006, October 26). In a seller's market, Cornell needs to recruit hundreds of new faculty, putting years-long pressure on budget. [Electronic Entry] Retrieved July 19, 2007, from http://www.news.cornell.edu/stories/DC.faculty.ws.html

Steiner, J. F., Curtis, P., Lanphear, B. P., Vu, K. O., & Main, D. S. (2004). Assessing the role of influential mentors in the research development of primary care fellows. *Academic Medicine, 79*(9), 865–872.

Strathe, M. L., & Wilson, V. W. (2006) Academic leadership: The pathway to and from. *New Directions for Higher Education, 134*, 5–13.

Stritter, F. T., Bland, C. J., & Youngblood, P. L. (1991). Determining essential faculty competencies. *Teaching and Learning in Medicine, 3*(4), 232–238.

Super, D. E. (1986). Life career roles: Self-realization in work and leisure. In D. T. Hall and Associates, *Career Development in Organizations* (pp. 95–119). San Francisco: Jossey-Bass.

Taylor, M. S., & Ilgen, D. R. (1981). Sex discrimination against women in initial placement decisions: a laboratory investigation. *Academy of Management Journal, 24*(4), 859–863.

Tenenbaum, H. R., Crosby, F. J., & Gliner, M. D. (2001). Mentoring relationships in graduate school. *Journal of Vocational Behavior, 59*(3), 326–341.

Teodorescu, D. (2000). Correlates of faculty publication productivity: A cross-national analysis. *Higher Education, 39,* 201–222.

Thomas, D. A. (1989). Mentoring and irrationality: The role of racial taboos. *Human Resource Management, 28*(2), 279–290.

Thomas, D. A. (2001). The truth about mentoring minorities: Race matters. *Harvard Business Review, 79*(4), 98–107.

Tierney, W. G., & Bensimon, E. M. (2002). Socialization and cultural taxation: Race and ethnicity in the academy. In C. S. Turner, A. L. Antonio, M. Garcia, B. V. Laden, A. Nora, & C. L. Presley (Eds.), *Racial and ethnic diversity in American higher education* (pp. 209–221). Boston: Pearson Custom Publishing.

Tschannen-Moran, M., Firestone, W. A., Hoy, W. K., & Johnson, S. M. (2000). The Write Stuff: A study of productive scholars in educational administration. *Educational Administration Quarterly, 36*(3), 358–390.

Tulgan, B. (2000). *Managing Generation X: How to bring out the best in young talent.* (Revised and updated). New York: W.W. Norton.

Turner, J. L., & Boice, R. (1987). Starting at the beginning: Concerns and needs of new faculty. In *To improve the academy* (Vol. 6, pp. 41–55). Stillwater, OK: New Forums Press.

U. S. Department of Education, & The National Center for Education Statistics (NCES) (2002). *1999 National Study of Postsecondary Faculty (NSOPF:99) Methodology Report. NCES 2002-154. by Sameer Y. Abraham, Darby Miller Steiger, Margrethe Montgomery, Brian D. Kuhr, Roger Tourangeau, Bob Montgomery, and Manas Chattopadhyay. Project Officer Linda J. Zimbler.* Washington, DC: US Department of Education, National Center for Education Statistics.

U. S. Department of Education, & The National Center for Education Statistics. 2004 Study of Postsecondary Faculty Data Analysis System. [Electronic Entry] Retrieved February 26, 2007, from http://nces.ed.gov/surveys/nsopf/das.asp.

Van Maanen, J., & Schein, E. H. (1979). Toward a theory of organizational socialization. *Research Organizational Behavior, 1,* 209–264.

Visart, N. (1979). Communication between and within research units. In F. Andrews (Ed.), *Scientific productivity: The effectiveness of research groups in six countries* (pp. 223–252). Cambridge, England: Cambridge University Press.

Wanberg, C. R., Kammeyer-Mueller, J., & Marchese, M. (2006). Mentor and protégé predictors and outcomes of mentoring in a formal mentoring program. *Journal of Vocational Behavior, 69*(3), 410–423.

Wanberg, C. R., Welsh, E. T., & Hezlett, S. A. (2003). Mentoring research: A review and dynamic process model. *Research in Personnel and Human Resources Management, 22*, 39–124.

Ward, K., & Wolf-Wendel, L. (2004). Fear factor: How safe is it to make time for family? *Academe, 90*(6), 28–31.

Wheeler, D. W., & Wheeler, B. J. (1994). Mentoring faculty for midcareer issues. In M.A. Wunsch (Ed.), *Mentoring revisited: Making an impact on individuals and institutions.* (New Directions for Teaching and Learning, No. 57, pp. 91–97). San Francisco: Jossey Bass.

Williams, R., & Blackburn, R. T. (1988). Mentoring and junior faculty productivity. *Journal of Nursing Education, 27*(5), 204–209.

Wilson, P. P., Pereira, A., & Valentine, D. (2002). Perceptions of new social work faculty about mentoring experiences. *Journal of Social Work Education, 38*(2), 317–333.

Wingard, D.L., Garman, K.A., & Reznik, V. (2004). Facilitating faculty success: Outcomes and cost benefits of the UCSD National Center of Leadership in Academic Medicine. *Academic Medicine, 79*(10 Suppl), S9–S11.

Wise, M. R., Shapiro, H., Bodley, J., Pittini, R., McKay, D., Willian, A. (2004). Factors affecting academic promotion in obstetrics and gynaecology in Canada. *Journal of Obstetrics and Gynaecology Canada, 26.* 127–136.

Wolf-Wendel, L., & Ward, K. (2006). Faculty work and family life: Policy perspectives from different motivational types. In S. J. Bracken, J. K. Allen, & D. R. Dean (Eds.), *The balancing act: Gendered perspectives in faculty roles and work lives* (pp. 51–72). Sterling, VA: Stylus Publishing, LLC.

Wolverton, M., Ackerman, R., & Holt, S. (2005). Preparing for leadership: What academic department chairs need to know. *Journal of Higher Education Policy and Management, 27*(2), 227–238.

Wolverton, M., Gmelch, W. H., Montez, J., & Nies, C. T. (2001). *The changing nature of the academic deanship.* ASHE-ERIC Higher Education Report, *28*(1). New York: John Wiley & Sons.

Wolverton, M., Gmelch, W. H., Wolverton, M. L., & Sarros, J. C. (1999). A comparison of department chair tasks in Australia and the United States. *Higher Education, 38*, 333–350.

Wunsch, M. A. (1993). Mentoring probationary women academics—a pilot programme for career development. *Studies in Higher Education, 18*(3), 349–362.

Wunsch, M. A. (Ed.) (1994). *Mentoring revisited: Making an impact on individuals and institutions* (New Directions for Teaching and Learning, No. 57). San Francisco: Jossey Bass.

Yedidia, M. J., & Bickel, J. (2001). Why aren't there more women leaders in academic medicine? The views of clinical department chairs. *Academic Medicine, 76*(5), 453–465.

Zachary, L. J. (2000). *The mentor's guide: Facilitating effective learning relationships.* San Francisco: Jossey-Bass.

Zachary, L. J. (2005). *Creating a mentoring culture: The organization's guide.* Hoboken, NJ: John Wiley & Sons, Inc.

Zey, M. G. (1984). *The mentor connection.* Homewood, IL: Dow Jones-Irwin.

Index

About the Authors

Carole J. Bland (1946–2008), **PhD,** was assistant dean for faculty development in the medical school, professor in the Department of Family Medicine and Community Health, Medical School, and member of the Department of Educational Policy and Administration, College of Education and Human Development, all at the University of Minnesota. In addition, she directed a three-year clinical research fellowship for training family medicine investigators and taught courses and workshops on education, administration, research, evaluation, mentoring, and faculty vitality. She served as a consultant in these areas, as well as on physician specialty choice, to departments, universities, foundations, professional associations, and the federal government. She served as chair of the board of directors of the Alfred Adler Graduate School, as a trustee for Augustana College, and chaired or served on numerous other organizational and editorial boards, national peer review committees, and task forces. Her research focused on the development and productivity of faculty, administrators, and institutions. She was series editor of the Springer Series on Medical Education and wrote one hundred publications, including an award-winning book, *The Vitality of Senior Faculty Members: Snow on the Roof—Fire in the Furnace* and her most recent book, *The Research-Productive Department: Strategies from Departments that Excel.* Dr. Bland passed away while this book was being prepared for publication. This book is dedicated in her honor.

Anne L. Taylor, MD, is vice dean for academic affairs at Columbia University Medical Center, College of Physicians and Surgeons where she oversees all faculty processes and programs. She was formerly professor of medicine/cardiology and associate dean for faculty affairs at the University of Minnesota Medical School. Dr. Taylor's research has focused on cardiovascular disease in African Americans and women. She chaired the Steering Committee for the African-American Heart Failure Trial, a national multicenter trial of nitric oxide-enhancing therapy in congestive heart failure. In her role as associate dean for faculty affairs at the University of Minnesota, Dr. Taylor initiated and led a restructuring of the medical school's academic tracks to better align them with mission-critical faculty activities and initiated the development of the faculty mentoring program, designed to support faculty in their varied roles. Dr. Taylor has codirected the jointly sponsored National Institutes of Health/National Medical Association collaborative career development seminar for minority fellows preparing for careers in academic medicine. In addition, she has collaborated with the University of Minnesota's Center of Excellence in American Indian and Minority Health and the American Association for American Indian Physicians in the development of an annual program titled Academic Medicine and Careers in Research for American Indian students. Dr. Taylor's activities within the University of Minnesota's Deborah E. Powell Center of Excellence in Women's Health were focused on the leadership component, which addresses the needs of women faculty.

S. Lynn Shollen, PhD, coordinates and teaches leadership development through the Centennial Center for Leadership at Hobart and William Smith Colleges in Geneva, NY. She earned her degree in higher education policy and administration from the University of Minnesota, where she was a graduate research assistant in the University of Minnesota Postsecondary Education Research Institute. Her assistantship was linked to the Department of Family Medicine and the Medical School Office of Faculty Affairs. Dr. Shollen's research interests include leadership development, mentoring as a leadership initiative, identity and perceptions of leadership, and organizational culture.

Anne Marie Weber-Main, PhD, is assistant professor and research medical editor in the University of Minnesota's Department of Medicine, where she applies her skills as a basic scientist, seasoned medical writer and editor, and teacher of scientific communication to support the research careers of faculty in the health sciences. She previously served as associate director of research in the University of Minnesota's Department of Family Medicine and Community Health. She has taught in the University of Minnesota's Medical School and School of Public Health on topics related to grant writing and writing for publication. She also serves as the writing consultant for assistant professors participating in the university's multidisciplinary Clinical Research Career Development Program, funded by a Roadmap K12 grant from the National Institutes of Health. Nationally, Dr. Weber-Main is a workshop leader in the core curriculum program of the American Medical Writers Association. Her publications are in the areas of research productivity, faculty mentoring, and biomedical communications. She is also a mentor of new medical writers.

Patricia A. Mulcahy, MBA, serves as the associate dean for strategic projects at the University of Minnesota Medical School. As a member of the dean's leadership team, she resolves administrative issues on behalf of the dean, contributes to the development of strategic initiatives, and interfaces with the Academic Health Center and campus offices on behalf of the medical school. She serves as a coordinator, facilitator, and negotiator with an emphasis on problem solving and finding innovative ways to address issues within the framework of established policies and procedures. Ms. Mulcahy represents the medical school on the University of Minnesota Improvement Liaison Group and as chair of the University's Human Resources Management System Steering Committee.

Made in the USA
Middletown, DE
02 September 2016